# HOME AT LAST

## Your Journey of Faith

## in Challenging Times

## RUTH PEARSON

# Published by

# Introducing

**ISBN:**9781838283803

**Book Cover Design:** Listening To Your Voice Publishing.

**Editor:** Ruth Pearson.

**Typesetters:** Ruth Pearson and Winsome Duncan.

**Proof-readers:** Linda Green and Joy Braithwaite.

# Contents

"This is my command—be strong and courageous!

Do not be afraid or discouraged.

For the LORD your God is with you wherever you go." *(Joshua 1:9)*

# Dedication

I would like to dedicate this book to you,
the reader.

God made a covenant to Abraham;
his descendants would occupy Canaan.
God has made a similar covenant with you.

God kept His word and the Children of Israel arrived
in Canaan with Joshua as their leader.

I pray, as you go on your own personal journey of
faith, 'Home at Last', will assist you in listening to
God's voice, as you travel to your eternal home!

# Acknowledgements

I would like to thank Father God for allowing me to go on a journey from being lame to walking, not just physically but also spiritually.

This journey has been the foundation of my more intimate and meaningful relationship, with God. This book is a celebration of six years of being transformed in my life since that miraculous day, in May 2014.

I would like to thank **Winsome Duncan** of **Peaches Publications** for her invaluable knowledge and support in establishing **Listening To Your Voice Publishing.**

I would like to thank my family and friends, both here in the UK and abroad, for your support and encouragement. It has progressively enriched our relationships over the years.

I would like to thank my church families, who have fed me spiritually over the years and encouraged me to continue writing, since the publishing of my first devotional book, **Listening for God's Voice: 40 Days of Developing Intimacy with God**.

I would like to thank Rosalind Lawless for her Dragon training, which has given me a new lease of life, so I can now use dictation, as well as typing, to share God's words of inspiration.

I would like to thank **Oneta Letang**, **Joy Braithwaite** and **Linda Green** for their invaluable input with editing and proofreading. The manuscript is more richer.

I would like to thank you, the reader. May you learn to listen to Father's voice as you read this book, and go on your own personal journey of faith, so one day, I pray, you can say, **"I'm Home at Last!"**

# Foreword

Ruth Pearson is an established author, speaker and a great ecclesiast of this day and age. I first met Ruth when she walked into my ministry many years ago and I saw the woman she has become today. She was about to venture into the deep. I was simply the push she needed at that time to start her own journey.

In her new book '**Home at Last'**, Ruth explains in detail how to start a journey and finish it well. Not all runners are winners, but all winners are runners. Ruth's tips, road markings and signs on the road will help you navigate each stage of your journey.

Life's journey is both physically and emotionally draining. While we all see the end, yet we can be short-sighted to the obstacles right in front of us. But Ruth has given us an every day manual, a prototype of what you can achieve.

Ruth coaches you through each step of your personal journey. She makes you know that you are not alone. This book will help you not only travel, but also enjoy each stage of the journey. It's not about getting there. It's about how you get there.

Shalom

**Snr Pastor Austin VJ Makota**

Bread of Life Church

# Introduction: The Journey

*"Are we leaving today? Are we leaving today?"* The children eagerly asked their parents this question, over and over again, as they saw preparations being made at home.

Unlike other days when they would get up and complete their chores at home, they were told to pack their bags with things they wanted to take with them. This special journey, they would be taking as a family. They would not be able to take all of their possessions, so they would have to choose wisely the essentials.

*"Where are we going?"* was the children's next question.

*"On a special journey,"* replied their parents.

*"A special journey?   What does that mean?"* continued the children.

*"A special journey.   That's all we know. We have been given strict instructions as to how we need to prepare and we're going to obey."*

*"What have you been asked to do?"* the children asked, full of excitement.

"We have been asked to choose a young lamb or a young goat, a year old, which has no defects, for a

1

sacrifice; one animal for each household. If the family is small the lamb must be shared with another family in the local neighbourhood.

At twilight, on the evening of the fourteenth day, of the first month, it must be killed. The elders need to drain the blood into a basin. Then they need to take a bundle of hyssop branches, dip it into the blood, and then brush the hyssop across the sides and top of the doorframes of the houses where we are gathered together as a family to eat the meal.

This same night, we must roast the meat of the whole lamb or goat, over a fire and eat it with bitter salad greens and bread made without yeast. We are not allowed to break any of its bones as we cook or eat it. If any of the meat is left after we have finished eating, it must be burnt, before the next morning.

Once the door is closed that night, no one may go through the door until morning. As a family we need to eat this meal with urgency. We have to be fully dressed, wearing a belt around our waist, having our sandals on our feet, and holding our walking sticks in our hands."

*"That's a lot of details we need to follow, but it must be important that we obey. What can we do to help? We want to do our part to obey God's commands too."* The children replied bubbling over with enthusiasm.

*This was the last night the family spent in their homes in Egypt, because at midnight, the angel of death passed over Egypt, and in every home, which did not make the preparations above, the firstborn son died, including Pharaoh's son.*

*In the night Pharaoh sent for Moses and Aaron, his brother, and said to them, "Get out! Leave my people and take the rest of the Israelites with you! Go and worship the LORD as you have requested. When you leave take your flocks and herds. Leave quickly, I do not want all of us to die!"* **(Exodus 12:31-33)**

*The Israelites took their bread dough before yeast was added. They wrapped their kneading boards in their cloaks and carried them on their shoulders. And the people of Israel did as Moses had instructed; they asked the Egyptians for clothing and articles of silver and gold. The LORD caused the Egyptians to look favourably on the Israelites, and they gave the Israelites whatever they asked for.* **So, they stripped the Egyptians of their wealth!** *That night the people of Israel left Rameses and started for Succoth. There were about 600,000 men, plus all the women and children.* **(Exodus 12:34-37)**

This was the beginning of their journey from Egypt to Canaan. The journey should have taken them 11 days, but because of a lack of faith and unwillingness to take the land, it took them 40 years to possess their promised homeland. A whole generation died on the way; only Joshua and Caleb crossed over the Red Sea and the River Jordan.

## Joshua as Leader

The time for the Israelites to go and occupy their new home had finally arrived. Just as before Israel left Egypt and God instructed Moses, He now gave instructions to Joshua, the new leader, about what they needed to do, in preparation to cross over the river Jordan into Canaan.

*"**I promise you what I promised Moses**: 'Wherever you set your foot, you will be on land I have given you— from the Negev wilderness in the south to the Lebanon mountains in the north, from the Euphrates River in the east to the Mediterranean Sea in the west, including all the land of the Hittites.' No one will be able to stand against you as long as you live. For I will be with you as I was with Moses. I will not fail you or abandon you.*

*"**Be strong and courageous**, for you are the one who will lead these people to possess all the land I swore to their ancestors I would give them. [7] Be strong and very courageous. Be careful to obey all the instructions Moses gave you. Do not deviate*

*from them, turning either to the right or to the left. Then you will be successful in everything you do.* **(Joshua 1:3-7)**

## God's Covenant

Why was this journey so significant for Joshua and the children of Israel?

The seed for this journey was planted years ago when God was having a conversation with Abraham. Abraham had been called by God to go on a journey of faith. When he was 75 years old, the LORD appeared to him and said He was going to make a covenant between Himself and Abram. At age 99 God repeated the promise to Abraham. In that conversation God said that He would change his name from Abram to Abraham and his wife Sarai to Sarah.

Why did God change their names?

To reflect their new identities! This was a time of new beginnings and a deeper, more intimate relationship with God.

In this covenant found in **Genesis 12:1-7 and Genesis 17,** God told Abraham that he would become the father of nations. his descendants would occupy a land in which he is now a stranger; ALL THE LAND of Canaan, would be given to them as an everlasting possession. If this blessing was not amazing enough, God also said to Abraham, He would always be their God. He would always want to have a good relationship with them.

God also said that Sarah at the age of 90 would now become the mother of a son, and Abraham would become a father at aged 100. This was not the time when individuals lived to be 900 years, so having a child at 100 was considered young. No! Sarah was past the child bearing age. But as they were to discover, God can do impossible things in their life, and He can do impossible things in your life too.

Not only would Sarah be the mother of a son, God gave her a promise also found in **Genesis 17:16**. God said that He would bless her, and she would become the mother of nations, and kings of people will be her descendants.

Just as God made this covenant promise, to Abraham, He has made a covenant with each one of us as His children. He wants to be our God and have an intimate relationship with us too. God has made His decision. You now have the choice to decide if you want to have a covenanted relationship with Him.

## Our Changed World

As we look around we can see a lot of changes have occurred in our world even before the pandemic (within families and communities, also politically, environmentally, financially, and socially).

If we are truly honest with ourselves, we knew deep within a change was needed. Things could not continue the way they were, with all of the pain, turmoil and challenges being experienced by the majority.

At the start of 2020, we would never have imagined that in less than three months, everyone's lives around the world would have changed as they did.

Who would ever have imagined that within a matter of days, flights would be cancelled, businesses would be closed, school children would be taught online, and families would be in lockdown, only allowed out to purchase food, collect medicines or to attend vital appointments?

The world at first was filled with so much fear, but then the fear turned into a strange sort of peace.

Many said, "It is as if a reset button has been pressed, and we have to start living life again, but in a different way. A way in which we think about the needs of others more, and live as a community, instead of, as individuals."

All around us we saw people doing random acts of kindness for their neighbours, or for people in need. An army of volunteers were mobilised to work in their local communities.

Many countries in the world were in conflict, before the lockdown, and many things were deteriorating. In 2020, these conflicts, took second place, with people focusing more on meeting basic needs, and staying healthy and alive.

Individuals were wondering, *"What do all of these changes mean?"*

*"What major event could be happening in the world?"*

Many wondered, *"Could these be the times of the end? Is it a precursor for the fulfilment of the promise that Jesus will come back to the earth, and that His coming is soon?"*

I believe these signs are the beginning of birth pains and are pointing us to the greatest event ever to happen in this Earth's history, the **Second Coming** of Jesus, as shared in His Word.

This event will be one of the fulfilments of many of the promises found in the Bible. The role of Jesus is promised in this covenanted relationship. "Immanuel" meaning, "God with us" is what God wants to have with us.

Jesus had to be born as a baby. He needed to come to this earth the first time, to fulfil the promises written about His life as found in the Psalms and written by the Bible prophets.

Jesus needed to come the first time to live a sinless life, die on the cross, in the place of each one of us. Jesus is coming again, the second time as a King, to take us as His children home with Him and so fulfil the covenant made with God, before time, as we know it, began on this earth.

At **Passover** we celebrate the journey the children of Israel took as they left Egypt and how the angel of death passed over the every home, that had blood on the doorposts, so that no firstborn son in their families died in the final plague, which fell. This meal was the one shared in the introduction to this book.

At **Easter** we celebrate Jesus' death on the cross and resurrection from the grave; the empty tomb. Jesus is the only person who has died that we do not refer to as, "The late…"

In **Acts 1:9-11, (KJV)** we read about His ascension to heaven and we are given the promise in verse 11,

"*This **same** Jesus, who was taken up from you into heaven, will so come in like manner as you saw Him go into heaven.*"

In **1 Thessalonians 5: 1-3 (KJV),** we have a description of the Day of the Lord, as written by the apostle Paul, which he says will take place, unexpectedly. While some mothers' now are able to plan the date of birth of their child(ren), due to improvement of modern medicine, the date of the 'Day of the Lord' cannot be unexpectedly planned by mankind.

*"But concerning the times and the seasons, brethren, you have no need that I should write to you. For you yourselves know perfectly that the day of the Lord so comes as a thief in the night. For when they say, "Peace and safety!" then sudden destruction comes upon them, as labour pains upon a pregnant woman. And they shall not escape."*

In **Revelation 19:16** we are told He will come again as the **KING OF KINGS AND LORD OF LORDS.** When He returns, He will set up His kingdom, the final one shown to Nebuchadnezzar, in his dream found in **Daniel 2:32-35**.

## Nebuchadnezzar's Dream

Nebuchadnezzar, the leader of Babylon, had a dream one night that troubled him. In his dream he saw a big statue made of different metals, gold, silver, bronze, iron, a mixture of iron and clay.

Nebuchadnezzar in his dream, then saw a stone cut out without hands, strike the image on its feet of iron and clay, and broke them into pieces. Then the iron, the clay, the bronze, the silver, and the gold became like chaff on the summer threshing floor. The wind blew the chaff away so that there was no trace of them found. The stone that struck the image became a great mountain and filled the whole earth.

Daniel, one of the great leaders, a captured prince taken to Babylon, went and prayed to God, with three of his friends and asked God what was the meaning of the dream. God revealed to Daniel the meaning of the dream.

Daniel went to the King, the next day, and said to him, *"There is a God in heaven who reveals secrets, and He has made known to you, King Nebuchadnezzar what will happen in the latter days."* **(Daniel 2:28 NKJV)**

We are living in these latter days of earth's history.

Nebuchadnezzar was shown all of the major kingdoms which will be on the earth, starting with Babylon, his kingdom, until to the end of time.

The **head of gold** represented **Babylon**. This kingdom lasted from 626 – 539 BC.

The **chest and arms of silver** represented **Medo-Persia**. This kingdom lasted from 539 – 331 BC.

The **belly and thighs of bronze** represented **Greece**. This kingdom lasted from 331 – 168 BC.

The **legs of iron** represented **Rome**. This kingdom lasted from 168 BC – A.D. 476.

The **feet partly of iron and partly clay** represents **divided kingdoms** after the fall of Rome and they will end with The Second Coming of Christ.

In 2020, we have **The Group of Seven** (G7), consisting of seven major developed counties: Canada, **France, Germany, Italy,** Japan, the **United Kingdom** and the United Stated, as an international intergovernmental economic organisation.

This organisation, truly shows us that some of the European countries (highlighted) as well as others in the world, represents these divided kingdoms of iron and clay, we are now living in.

When King Nebuchadnezzar, watched the dream unfold, the final kingdom was shown as a stone which struck the image at the feet.

*"You watched while a stone was cut out without hands, which struck the image on its feet of iron and clay, and broke them in pieces. Then the iron, the clay, the bronze, the silver, and the gold were crushed together, and became like chaff from the summer threshing floors; the wind carried them away so that no trace of them was found. And the*

*stone that struck the image became a great mountain and filled the whole earth." (Daniel 2:34-35 NLT)*

No wonder King Nebuchadnezzar was terrified when he had this dream that no one could interpret, until he was directed to Daniel.

History has shown that all the kingdoms King Nebuchadnezzar saw in his dream have happened in the right sequence, and with the power shown.

As a result, we can be confident the final part of this dream of the stone that was cut out without hands, that struck the image on its feet of iron and clay, will become a great mountain and fill the whole earth.

**Time of Preparation**

When a mother experiences the first contraction pains, she begins to make the final preparations at home for the arrival of her new-born baby. As the contraction pains get stronger and stronger and closer together, she waits with anticipation knowing she will soon give birth to her baby boy or girl. The birth pains are a sign new changes will be taking place in the near future.

This is similar to what we are seeing happening in society. We had the initial pains, episodes of unrest here or there, but didn't understand something important was happening. We did not understand their significance. The pains have gotten stronger and stronger and now they are reaching the point of no return. As they continue, we know birth has to take place soon. We just do not know how much longer we will have on planet earth, as we now know it, before Jesus' Second Coming.

## The Days of Noah!

As a child you probably heard or read the story of the animals going into an ark two by two, so they would not be destroyed by the rain which was going to fall on the land. Rain was something new, as the ground was watered by dew.

How did Noah know that he needed to build an ark and the dimensions of it? How did he know God's plan for the people who were living on the earth? God spoke with Him.

As God looked at the actions of the men living on the earth, He was sorry that He had made man on the earth and it grieved His heart **(Genesis 6:6)**. The majority of people did not want to have a relationship with Him, they did not think this was important in their life. They just wanted to have fun and do things their own way instead of God's way.

14

So, God decided He would destroy everyone alive except for Noah and his family and two of most of the species of animals, a male and a female.

To save them, Noah was asked to build a large boat called an Ark. This Ark was to keep them safe from external dangers. Everyone would be warned about the dangers coming and they would have to decide if they wanted to be inside the Ark, or continue their lives as they had always lived them. Unfortunately, the people did not listen to the warning given to them by Noah of the immediate danger and so they died when the rains came.

**Lockdown!**

At the start of 2020, we never would have imagined we too would have to make a choice to stay in our homes, unless we are making essential journey, or was a Keyworker, or continue life as usual without changing our behaviour.

The first few days at home, was as if we were having some family indoor time. But the days turned to weeks and the weeks to months.

The things which were important in life, before the lockdown, lost their appeal as families were at home waiting, and wondering how long it would be before they could leave their homes and go and socialise with extended family and friends again.

We can imagine how Noah felt when he was in the ark, alone with his immediate family and the animals, wondering how long it would be before he could leave his 'lockdown' and go back out on land.

As I typed the original copy of this, the date is the **27th March 2020**, and the beginning of the Sabbath day as shared in **Exodus 20:8-11**; sunset has just taken place.

It is the first Sabbath, Saturday, the majority of shops are closed, the majority of planes are grounded, places of entertainment are closed, hotels are closed, and there is a sense of stillness in the air. This lockdown is not just here in the UK, where I live, but in the majority of countries around the world. Even my family in Barbados are going on lockdown from today until at least the beginning of May 2020.

Each day, there are news updates of the number of deaths occurring locally and globally because of the pandemic. But in the midst of this crisis there has been an awakening of the conscience.

Individuals are seeking guidance and comfort from God. Individuals who in the past did not believe God existed, are now turning to Him for help. Doctors who thought science had all of the answers are realising they need help from a higher, divine, source.

What about you? How important is God in your life? Do you have a relationship with Him, like the one Nicodemus spoke about?

Nicodemus was a Pharisee, a member of the Jewish ruling council. He was part of the inner circle of the religious organisations of his day.

Despite the theoretical knowledge he had, he knew something was missing is his life. To maintain his position and reputation, he came to see Jesus at night, with a question.

**"What must I do to be saved?"**

"What must I do to have a close relationship with God?"

Jesus' response was one of the most familiar verses in the Bible,

*"For God so loved the world, that He gave His only begotten Son, that whosoever believeth in Him should not perish, but have everlasting life" (John 3:16 KJV).*

## The Arrival of the Comforter

After the death of Jesus and His ascension into heaven, the disciples went back to the upper room and remained locked in there, because they feared for their lives. Jesus had also told them they should remain together as a group because He was going to send them a special gift, the gift of the Holy Spirit also called The Comforter **(John 14:26 KJV).**

This Comforter shall teach them all things, and bring all things to remembrance which Jesus had taught them.

They sat in the room for 10 days. They had time to mend relationships, to ask for forgiveness from each other for previous pain and misunderstandings, and time to pray. As they waited, they heard a loud sound like rushing wind.

"What was happening?"

In **Acts 2**, we read about the birth of the new church and the outpouring of the Holy Spirit. The disciples and all of those who were gathered in the upper room, had tongues of fire rest upon their heads. This act, changed their lives in remarkable ways.

They were able to speak new languages and shared about their personal experiences of being with Jesus to the crowd which had gathered outside of the room they were staying in.

The crowd was attracted to the loud noise that came from their room. The crowd was amazed at what they were seeing and hearing, as they knew these men had been fishermen, and were not learned men.

On this day, which is called the **Day of Pentecost**, Peter stood up and spoke. As he spoke, the people listening to him were cut to the heart and said to Peter and the rest of the apostles, *"What shall we do to be saved?"*

They listening crowd naturally wanted to respond to what they were hearing, as they felt the impact of the Holy Spirit within them. The response: 3000 men were baptised in one day. These men then became filled with the Holy Spirit, and the baton of the Good News was passed on.

In one day, so many lives were transformed. These 3000 men continued their journey of faith as followers of Jesus. Their life as Christians had started unexpectedly. They had a miraculous story to share with their family and friends, and their local communities.

### The Holy Spirit Will Be Poured Out Again

God has promised us in His Word, similar events will take place before Jesus' Second Coming, like what took place in the book of Acts. The Holy Spirit will be poured out on all those who will accept God into their life.

This outpouring of the Holy Spirit, before Jesus comes back, will be called The Latter Rain. The

Former Rain started to fall on the Day of Pentecost in the lives of the disciples, and those who were in the upper room.

Just as two seasons of rain are needed for a plant to develop and be ready to be harvested, the same will happen spiritually in the world. We read about this in **Joel 2:23.**

"*Be glad then you children of Zion, And rejoice in the Lord your God, For He has given you the former rain faithfully, And He will cause the rain to come down for you- The former rain, And the letter rain in the first month.*"

When this rain pours out over the earth, individuals will be given a choice, accept God into their life or reject Him. They will no longer be able to sit on the fence.

They will be like the two thieves who were crucified with Jesus. One accepted the gift of Jesus' sacrifice and the other rejected the gift. Both had the same opportunity; they just needed to make their own choice, to reject or accept the gift.

Many, during their time of lockdown turned to reading the Bible, to understand what was happening on the Earth. There was a time of deep searching and shaking.

Many were discovering who God was, and the relationship He wants with them as His children.

They are making the decision, to go on a journey of faith. For many, reading their Bible or listening to spiritual videos on audio was a new experience, and they may need some encouragement and guidance.

This is one of the reasons for writing this book; to give you some encouragement and to answer many life questions which may be in your thoughts and mind.

Perhaps you may be confused and overwhelmed by Covid-19. This pandemic now may have left you feeling far away from God, whereas in the past, you had a closer and more intimate relationship. You now may be reflecting on the steps you can take to get back home. You want to know how you can now have a closer and deeper relationship with "The Father".

If you may have been a church goer for decades, but challenges in life have left you feeling angry and bitter, you too may need to know how you can return home, into the arms of a loving Father, where you belong.

## The Doomsday Clock

We do not know how much time we have left before the stone, described in **Daniel 2**, will hit the earth.

The Doomsday Clock has been maintained since 1947. It is a clock which acts as a symbol to represent the likelihood of a man-made global disaster.

In 2017 it was 2 ½ minutes to midnight but in 2018 the time was changed to 2 minutes to midnight. In January 2020 it was changed to the smallest time of 100 seconds, (1 minute and 40 seconds) to midnight, based on increased threat to global stability.

## Natural Disasters

It is not only the Doomsday Clock that is telling us time is running out. A week did not pass, in 2019, without us hearing in the news of some natural disaster, or tragedy, which had resulted in a significant loss of life of individuals or property.

*"Do you think these disasters could be a warning to us of imminent danger to our planet?"*

Sir David Attenborough is a British Broadcaster and has produced many series about nature and the fine balance of life on earth. In his recent interviews and series, he reminded us we are running out of time due to climate change and the need to put into place strategies to look after the earth's natural resources.

It appears we are getting the same message from a variety of sources. "Are we listening? Really listening?"

## Three Important Questions

With all of this evidence from multiple places, I have a few direct, important questions to ask you, dear reader. I believe the answers you give to these questions will impact your life, not just for the short time you live on earth, but eternally.

Here are my three questions?

1. **How important is God in your life?**
2. **Do you have a personal relationship with God?**
3. **Where are you planning to spend eternity?**

These questions form the basis of this book, and you will see them asked many times. We are reminded in **Ecclesiastes 3:11**

*"He has made everything beautiful in its time. Also, He has put eternity in their hearts, except that no one can find out the work that God does from beginning to end."*

For some, a relationship with God is an integral part of their life journey. To others God plays no part in their life. The latter, openly reject the relationship God wants to have with them. Many do not believe God or the devil even exists.

On the journey home, some forget there is always a good person and an evil person as portrayed in many good plots or stories.

One a scale of **0 to 10**, where **0** are those individuals who say God does not exist to **10,** they know, 100%, He exists, because they have a daily living relationship with Him; where are you on this scale?

Would you say that you are somewhere in the middle between **2** to **8**?

The score you have given yourself, will be your starting point in your own personal journey of faith.

My prayer for you is as you read this book, it will transform your life. I pray by the time you read the final word on the last page, you will have developed a deeper relationship with Father God, and your faith will have grown, by your score moving closer to 10.

When you have completed your journey, I want you to be able to say these words, or similar ones, that the apostle Paul shared with Timothy when he knew he was facing death.

*"I have fought the good fight, I have finished the race, I have kept the faith. Finally, there is laid up for me the crown of righteousness, which the Lord, the righteous Judge, will give to me on that Day, and not to me only but also to all who have loved His appearing,"* **(2 Timothy 4: 7-8 NLT).**

I pray when your journey of faith comes to an end, you and all who consciously go on their own journey of faith, will receive their crowns of righteousness. There are more than enough crowns for every one of us!

# CHAPTER 1

## *Let's Get Started*

I get really excited, when starting a new project or I am going on a new journey. What about you?

If someone was to ask you the question, "**How important is God in your life?**" How would you respond? On the scale of **0 to 10** what number did you give your relationship with Him?

Everything must have a starting point and also an end point. Most starting points begin with a thought in your mind, which you may write down or make a note in your conscious mind.

You may even share the thought with others who you trust, or get advice about them. You may then put into place actions to explore how you can make what you were thinking about, become a reality.

This book started as a thought in my mind. I had a few ideas about how to write it, based on previous books I had written, but the original version of this book was extra special because it was not planned; it unfolded as I sat at my laptop.

I had to make the decision to type the thoughts given or ignore them. If I had not acted on the thoughts, then you would not have had the opportunity to be reading this book, because it would not have existed.

My prayer, is as you read this book, you will go on your own personal journey of faith. The first five chapters will give you the tools to develop your own personal "road map" or relationship with Father God and chapters 6 to 10 will show you the blessings that come by sharing the journey with others.

Before I continue writing this book, let me pause and clear up a big misconception which some people believe. **Being on this journey of faith, will not negate you from having challenges in your life.**

If I am really honest, you may feel as if you are being attacked, from multiple places, even more, once you openly decide to go on this journey of faith, and the truth be told, you probably are.

But be reassured, as you go on this journey, you are not alone. There are others who are on a similar path who will be there to encourage and support you. There is also the comfort and joy you will get on this journey from the presence of the Holy Spirit.

There will be times when you may feel alone. At those times, you can always go to Father God, and tell Him honestly how you are feeling. This is where you open your heart in prayer, to God.

As you open up to Him, don't be surprised, if you get a call, from a friend, saying you were suddenly on their mind, so they picked up the phone to call you, or some other random act of kindness comes your way.

God wanting to have a personal relationship with you is special, through some think it is nothing new. It started right in the Garden of Eden.

In Genesis chapter one, we read about the birth of the heavens and the earth and all of their content; the birth of mankind and the family unit; and the birth of God having a relationship with His created beings. The book, called Genes(is), tells us the history of the human race through genes. Biologist remind us genes are the building blocks of life. What a fitting name!

In **Genesis 3:8a**, we are told in the cool of the day, God would come and converse with Adam and Eve. He still wants to have quality time with you, just in a different way.

The way you communicate is in prayer – which may be strange at first. Prayer is in effect, having a conversation with God, in a similar way as when you speak with a close friend.


**The Prodigal Son**

Fast forward about 4000 years and we have Jesus being born as a baby. We do not hear much about what happened in His early life until he was 30, when He started His ministry.

The purpose of His life, on earth, and His teachings were to reveal more to us about the true character of God, His Father; Our Father. He showed to us in practical ways, God is a Good Father, who wants a loving relationship with His children, and that includes you; as you are His child.

There are many stories, or parables, in the Bible which show a real picture of God's love. One such story, which many know and can relate to, is the story of **The Prodigal Son** as found in **Luke 15:11- 32**.

In the next few chapters, I will be using aspects of this story as an illustration of this journey of faith you are on, until you arrive home at last!

At the start of the story, we have a family. A father with his two sons. The younger son decided he wanted his inheritance, whilst the father was still alive.

Although this decision caused the father great pain, the father gave the younger son what he asked for. The younger son, truly, did not value the gift, or the sacrifices the father had made in his life.

In a short period of time, the younger son was left with nothing, because of the poor decisions he made. He now had a final choice to make, stay where he was or return home; not as a son, but as a hired servant.

The younger son, decided to return home. One day he made the conscious decision to start to walk home. It would have taken courage to overcome doubt and to not listen to the negative voices in his head; Great courage!

As he started the journey home, he never imagined it story, would have been so difficult.

In his mind, he kept wondering what would others think of him. "*I let my father down. I let myself down. I let my family down.*"

With each step, he would have new negative thoughts, based on his past actions. Yet determined to get home, he pressed on.

Eventually he passed halfway in the journey. With each reluctant step, he was closer to home than away. He kept walking one step at a time. Hungry. Tired. Destitute and Disappointed, with himself.

In the horizon, he faintly saw the outline of a person coming in his direction. Or is it a mirage? As he looked closely, his dusty eyes could see, a person not walking but running. Was this a figment of his imagination?

Who could be in such a hurry to get to their destination, on such a long dusty road? He wondered. As the distance between them got shorter, parched, hungry and dehydrated, he looked up and realised the person running toward him was his father. Fainted and exhausted, he perked up. His father had come to story, get him, to bring him back home.

They embraced. The father was overjoyed to see him. He never thought they would have this reunion. The whole time, in his mind, his son was dead. He died the day he left home!

Both the son and the father were on their own at the start of the day. Now they were going back home as two. The son had left home alone, now his father was walking by his side. What a blessing. What love!

On his return, the father gave him new clothes to wear, a new identity and threw a welcome home party. He excitedly tells everyone in the community, "*My son was lost but now he is found. Let's celebrate!*"

The son had a choice whether to accept the gifts and treatment the father gave to him; fortunately, he did.

On the other hand, when the father asked his eldest son to join the party, he refused. He told his father about all the things he had done and reminded him no party was ever thrown for him. This eldest son was driven by actions and not by relationship. He did not realise relationship was the key to the celebration taking place.

It was sad to read that no matter how much the father asked the eldest son to join the celebration, this son refused to attend. I am sure this caused the father more pain than when the younger son left home!

## How Does This Parable Relate to You?

We are all part of one big family, the family of God. No matter what your background is, we are all one family.

Our Father loves us all individually and collectively. Some of us, like the younger son, demanding our inheritance, of free choice, early. Although it caused the Father pain, the Father allowed you to make your own decisions; as He created you with the gift of free choice. He does not force you to have a relationship with Him. It has to be your daily choice.

However, there may come a time in your life, when you may look around and realise you do not like where your choices in life has taken you.

Is this you?

As you reflect, you like the prodigal son may literally or figuratively run out of options and have nothing left.

You may remember about the times you had made good choices or had Father in your life. In your times of quiet reflection you think about the quality of your life now, and the quality of what your life could have been if you had made different choices. You also reflect on the quality of the lives of others, who lived with you at home.

You realise even as a servant things would be far better for you than they currently are. You then make the decision to return home; to take this journey of faith to re-join the family. You don't expect to be taken back as a son; you hope to be taken back as a servant.

This journey of reconciliation!

You start the journey home. It has taken a lot of courage to overcome doubt and to not listen to the negative voices in your head; Great courage!

Every step towards Father seems very difficult. You wonder what will others think, about this decision you have taken to live your life in a different way. What would Father do? Will He accept you, or send you away?

As you journey, these words, or similar thoughts, may come into your mind. "*I have let My Father down. I have let myself down.*" With each step, new thoughts come into your head, but you keep putting one foot in front of the other and persevere.

## The Importance of Perseverance

I know, even with these negative thoughts, it may be difficult to fathom your next step. How can you focus, think, and clear your head? Keep reading and keep moving forward. You are doing really well, because as you read these words you are growing mentally, spiritually and emotionally.

Keep walking towards your goal.

Keep walking!

Eventually you will pass halfway in your journey. You are not just thinking about, *"Should I go home?"* You can be proud, because you are moving towards your destination. You are closer to home than away. Keep walking, one step at a time!

On the horizon, you can see the outline of a person coming in your direction. As you look closely, you can see they are not walking but running. You wonder who is in such a hurry to get to their destination on this long dusty road.

As the distance between you gets shorter, you look up and realised the person running toward you, is Your Heavenly Father. Your Father has come to get you, to bring you back home.

Your Father gives you new clothes to wear, a new identity and throws a party for you. He tells everyone,

*"My child was lost but now he or she is found. Let's celebrate!"*

You must be feeling happy inside as you realise you made the right decision to keep reading on, as you are now making good progress in your journey.

## Love, Not Force is the Key!

While Father leaves you celebrating with the servants and others in the community, He goes to look for the elder child or children and asks then to come and join the celebration, but it breaks His heart when they refuse.

They tell the Father about all the good things they have done and no celebration was thrown for them. He reminds them, He loves them too and wants them to be part of the celebration. They refuse to join in, because they like the brother of the Prodigal, do not realise it is not "good" actions but an "intimate" relationship, which is at the core of our Father's Love. Love, not force, is the key to a lasting relationship.

None of us are perfect. We all make mistakes in our life. But God is running towards you with open forgiving arms, saying, *"My child, welcome home. Look at all of the preparations I have made for you: clothes, food, a home, and a lasting relationship. Let's celebrate!"*

What choice are you going to make?

Accept His gifts, or reject them!

I hope you will accept God's gifts as you continue your journey and say, "**I am heading home at last!**"

# CHAPTER 2

## *The Importance of Teamwork*

Have you ever seen a picture of the internal organs of the human body? As a science teacher, I am amazed how all of the organ systems work together. Each organ has its own design and function.

The **brain** works to coordinate how all the organs in the body work, and, it is the place where all our thoughts originate.

The **heart** to pump blood around the body, connected to arteries, capillaries and veins.

The **stomach**, to break down the food we eat into a liquid, similar to how a food blender works, as well as a defence mechanism to get rid of pathogens which may be in the food we eat.

The **kidneys** which filter our blood to get rid of toxins.

The **liver** a multi-tasked factory, making new chemicals like bile. The liver uses raw materials in new ways. It uses the amino acids from the breakdown of the many sources of proteins we take in our diet and transforms them to make new proteins in a variety of forms the body can use, including hormones, enzymes, keratin to make hair, nails, teeth, skin and antibodies.

You may not have seen the internal organs, only the external ones.

Our hands, fingers, feet, toes all have their own roles.

Our five senses, sight, touch, taste, hearing and smell, work separately, and together, to help us make sense of our environment.

## You Cannot do it Alone!

Just the same way the organs and organ systems need to work together so the body can be healthy and free from disease, so we must work together with each other holistically to ensure we are all healthy.

When the prodigal son arrived home, the father called those who knew the family, to come and celebrate the return of his younger son. They celebrated as a community.

We are all part of several communities: our immediate family; extended family; the neighbourhood we live in; the places we work or study; and, our places of worship. With the use of social media, we are also members of several online groups. Being a member of these real or virtual groups, we realise we have to work alongside others. We have to be part of a team. We are not an island.

## The Example of Jesus

When Jesus started His main ministry, on earth, He called others to work with Him. Andrew heard John the Baptist, say *"Behold the Lamb of God!"* as recorded in **John 1:35.** He then called his brother Simon Peter and said, *"We have found the Messiah, which is translated, the Christ"*. Philip and Nathaniel were called the next day.

On the third day, Jesus attended a wedding in Cana of Galilee and turned water into wine. It was there we find the story of his mother, Mary, telling the servants to do whatever He told them to do.

The instruction to fill up the water jugs used for the purification of the Jews was strange. They knew they were not going to use the water to be poured into basins to wash feet or clean hands, those tasks had already been completed.

So, what was the water going to be used for, once the empty jars were filled?

As they filled the large jugs, they did not understand the purpose, but as an act of faith they obeyed.

When they were told to draw some of the water out and take it to the master of the feast, they still had more questions than answers. But then, the miracle took place before their very eyes.

An act of faith, of drawing out the water and taking the first step towards the master of the feast changed their lives. They saw water become wine. The colour changed. The smell changed. The taste changed. The sounds around them changed all because they obeyed Jesus, by putting the spoon in the water and drawing it out for the Master of the feast to drink.

## How Does This Story Relate to You?

You may have started a journey. It may not have been this journey to get to know God better. Whatever the journey, you realise you cannot do this on your own. Just as Jesus called his first disciples to be with Him, we too need others to support us.

We cannot do things on our own. Jesus performed his first miracle at a wedding. He wanted to remind us of the importance that we cannot do everything on our own and about the importance of family celebrations, whoever you deem as 'your family'.

He wanted to remind us that when He returns and take us home, part of the preparations He is making for us now is to attend a wedding banquet. At this celebration, we will be able to share the event with all who have decided they too want to have an intimate relationship with God.

You may feel totally empty like the jars before they were filled with water. You may feel totally empty, thirsty, hungry and wasted, like the prodigal, before he went home.

As you go through this journey on earth, God may tell you to carry out strange requests like filling the empty jugs with water. Filling your jars may be repetitive and tedious. It may involve some spillage and mopping up.

Would you have filled the empty jars?

Like the servants at the wedding in Cana, you are being told right now to carry out tasks which do not make sense to you initially, but as you obey, you too may find what was empty in your life becomes full. By repetition, by spilling your hurts and pains to God, you know He can mop up your tears, wipe up your spillages and refill the emptiness in your life, to the brim,

**The Importance of Baptism**

Now you are filled, you are told to do something publicly, as an act of faith, to show others what you have been doing in the background. This for many is the act of baptism.

## What is Baptism?

Baptism is a ceremony which takes place when an adult or child is fully immersed in water, usually prayed for and assisted by a church leader. This act symbolises the end of the old life and the beginning of a new life.

It is also a symbol of Christ's burial and resurrection. Jesus gave us this example when He too was baptised by John in the river Jordan.

At a baptism service family and friends who have they seen the transformed life of the candidate usually shares with others why they have received the invitation to celebrate this special baptismal day with them.

After this celebration, the candidate(s) are formally welcomed a part of a church group to start the next phase of their spiritual journey.

You may not have taken this journey before in the past, and now you are at a crossroad. Perhaps you may have taken this step in the past and was baptised.

Wherever you may be on your journey, you may have chosen your own way, as the prodigal son did. I know some who have returned 'home' have asked to be re-baptised, whilst others have a special prayer of recommitment to show their new life direction.

From this stage in the journey, they are encouraged to spend quality time building up this intimate relationship, which is now at a deeper level, with God. This will involve a regular time of personal devotion. During this time, you can read from the Bible, or other faith-based book, and have a special time of prayer. Prayer is like talking to a friend but this friend is our Heavenly Father God.

Depending who is in your life, you can then have a devotional time with family members. You can even share devotionals with others via social media. I know I have benefitted from the encouragement shared by others and I know others have benefited from the encouragement I have shared with them, via social media. I have my own Facebook group, **Promise Verse for Today,** where I share devotionals with others.

You have now had the opportunity to take the first two steps on this journey of faith.

1.   Have you made the decision to have a deeper relationship with God?

2.    Have you shared this decision with others in a public way?

If you have not, would you like to make these decisions now?

If you're not ready you can skip over the next paragraphs so you can continue reading the rest of this book.

## Pray These Words!

*"God, I have not had a relationship with you in the past, but I now would like to have a new relationship with you, so I can call you Father.*

*Father God, thank you for wanting to have a relationship with me, even when I did not have one with you. Thank you for sending Your Son Jesus Christ to this world so that as I believe in Him, I shall not perish, but have eternal life.*

*I have done and thought and said bad things in the past, and I am sorry. I am asking you to forgive me.*

*I know Jesus is the only way to God. I now acknowledge He is the way, the truth and the life.*

*In the name of Jesus, I pray.*

*Amen."*

# Home at Last

# CHAPTER 3

## *Be Real with Your Emotions*

Let's return to the story of the prodigal son. We read in **Luke 15:17**, "*He came to himself*". He connected to his emotions.

He realised he did not like the situation he found himself in.

His father's servants were living a better quality of life than he was currently living.

He was prepared to be a servant, because he no longer saw his worth as a son.

He would apologise for his actions.

He arose and started on his journey home, to be with his father.

We also read in **Luke 15: 28** about the emotions of the eldest son, "*But he was angry and would not go in.*"

### The Importance of Being Real

If someone was to ask you the question, "*How are you feeling?*" Nine times out of ten you will respond, "*I am feeling fine.*" However, there are many times when

46

you are not feeling fine and wish there was someone there to support you. I know that you cannot be real with everyone, and share your innermost feelings with all, but it's important for your wellbeing that you have at least one person you can confide in, and be honest about your emotional health and wellbeing.

## Jesus' Disciples

In the previous chapter, we read about how Jesus chose his first disciples. He chooses 12 disciples, **(Luke 6:12-16)** who were His core team. He sent out the 12 and gave them their mission. He gave the disciples strict instructions about how they should prepare for this journey, **(Luke 9:6)**.

Jesus continued His ministry healing the sick, feeding 5000 men besides women and children, and as a result other disciples came to join His mission.

The number of disciples increased so eventually He had 70 **(Luke 10:1),** to send out to neighbouring towns and villages to make preparation for His arrival. What was the impact of their journey? Then the seventy returned with joy, saying, "*Lord, even the demons obey us when we use your name!*" (**Luke 10:17).**

## The Example of Jesus

In many of the stories in the Bible we are told Jesus took, Peter, James and John, his inner core with Him when He had special things to do. John had an even closer relationship with Him and was often referred to as the disciple Jesus loved. He also showed us the importance of supporting our loved ones. When He died on the cross, He asked John to look after his mother.

If Jesus, set this example for us, it is good practice for us to follow.

## Obstacles in the Journey

I am going to be real now. As you go on this journey of faith, obstacles are going to be placed in your way to slow you down. You may even have to stop for a while, depending on what the obstacle is. Not everyone is going to be happy with the choices you have made and the new direction your life is going in. Not everyone is going to be joyful. Some may even be angry as the prodigal son's older brother.

When you face these obstacles be real with yourself, and go and share your feelings with trusted friends to get supported.

## The Importance of Crying

One of the biggest obstacles that slows us down, is when we lose a loved one. For many days or weeks, it is as if our mind is in a fog. We go through the daily routines, but find it hard to connect with others, because of the grief we are feeling inside.

If you feel like crying at these times, cry. At a funeral I attended, the pastor told the family in particular, but all of us who attended, we need to weep for our loved ones. We need to express our emotions. *"Do not bottle them up. Crying is a way to express our emotions and crying will bring healing."*

As we cry, we're able to release some of the inner pain, and connect with our real emotions. Grief is a process; which individuals go through in their own way. So, if you're going through grief at this time, be kind to yourself!

We need to take the advice of Solomon found in **Ecclesiastes 3:1-4,** there is a time for everything under the sun, including a time to be born, a time to die, a time to weep and a time to laugh, a time to mourn, and a time to dance.

## The Importance of Forgiveness

Forgiveness is the intention of voluntarily pardoning someone who has caused you distress, either knowingly or unknowingly. It is not forgetting what they have done to you, but you decide how you want to progress with the rest of your life. Following the time of forgiveness, the individuals involved may rebuild their relationship or decide to part amicably.

Sometimes there is no amicable decision, because there can't be, particularly in the case of abuse, sometimes you forgive the abuser, and walk away because it is the safe thing to do for you mental health and self-worth.

When others have hurt you, you have the choice, whether or not you will be bitter, or better, because of the experience.

We find many examples of Jesus offering forgiveness to others, which annoyed many of the leaders observing Him. We find His ultimate example as He hung on the cross when He said in **Luke 23:34a, "Father, forgive them, for they don't know what they are doing."**

Doctors are finding many diseases are linked to unforgiveness, and pent up emotions that the person have not been able to share. If the patients seek emotional and spiritual support, they are able to see a big change in their conditions. Blood pressure decreases. Weight stabilises. Blood sugar stabilises. They no longer suffer from insomnia and need medication to help them to sleep. As they observe their own face in a mirror, they can see a face of peace looking back!

## How Does this Relate to Me?

When you go through various seasons of life, you share these with others.

As you go along this journey of faith, you are going to share your experiences with others.

As you go along your own personal journey, changes will happen. First you will have your own personal revival, when you make the decision to start this journey with God. This decision will impact your life, in many ways – places you visit, the language you use, the things you eat and drink, because you are making different choices.

These new choices are being observed by others, especially those closest to you. The changes were at first internal but now they can be seen externally by others.

In time, you will become connected with others who are on a similar journey. Over a period of time, you will choose some to become close friends, with whom you will share inevitably share your inner feelings and emotions.

Your trusted friends, will become like Peter, James and John, were to Jesus. In time, within this inner group, you will start to share your real emotions within this confidential inner group. This is how you will be supported, especially, when you face obstacles in your way.

## The Importance of Prayer

When you share your challenges, and are real, you will find these close friends will want to encourage you by praying with you and for you. They can share Bible promises, for you to claim for each challenge  you are going through. Reading and claiming these promises, as prayers, will strengthen you even more. A good place to start is with the Psalms.

King David who wrote many of the Psalms was able to express his emotions in an honest way. Find a version of the Bible that you can connect with well and why not pause to read **Psalm 143**. This psalm gives me comfort and I have found the heading '**An Earnest Appeal for Guidance and Deliverance**' relevant for the challenging times we are living in.

Other Psalms for encouragement are **Psalm 23**, **Psalm 27, Psalm 46** and **Psalm 91**. Once you start to read these you will find ones of your own to read.

## Who is God to You?

At times, there may be occasions, you just need to have some time alone, with God, so you can be fully open, honest and real by letting Him know how you really feel and what is on your mind.

Let me share my own experience with you to illustrate this point. One week in church, a sermon was preached on Jesus attending the wedding in Cana, as previously described, with his disciples. Remember the part Mary told the servants to do exactly what her Son told them to do.

At the end of the sermon, the preacher told me to go home and pour out my heart to God and share with Him how I was feeling about the challenges I was facing, which were many. She said if I felt angry tell Him, because He already knew.

I did not have a relationship with God in this way, at the time, so it felt strange at first. I had been taught I must respect my elders, and I had an even greater respect for God.

Was it respect or fear?

It took a while and several attempts, before I became real before God, and was able to pour out my heart to Him. There was a lot of crying, but in the end a sense of peace came over me, together with inner healing. I picked up a pen and paper and described how I was feeling, and I described who God was now to me.

These actions changed our relationship, from one where I knew about Him, like I know about the Queen of England, or another person in the media, to one of knowing Him intimately for myself.

I would encourage you to take some time out, so you can write or record your own list of who God is to you. You too may go on an emotional journey, but be assured in the end you will have peace; a peace money cannot buy.

# CHAPTER 4

## *Have A Positive Mindset*

In the past we were encouraged to look after our physical health by having a healthy diet which included having at least five pieces of different fruit and vegetables in the diet daily. There are many health related campaigns in the UK about improving diet, and they are even getting children involved in making healthy choices with apps or other incentives.

Families are also being encouraged to eat more whole grain foods; reduce the amount of unsaturated fat, sugar and salt, and eat less processed foods, by cooking fresh meals as a family, using raw ingredients. They are also being encouraged to drink more water to hydrate the body, because too many people are dehydrated.

The examples above are ways to improve physical health, but we are also hearing and reading, in the media, examples about how we can improve our emotional and mental wellbeing.

Many people of influence are sharing their stories, of how they have coped with anxiety and depression, and encouraging others to do the same, to get help in the beginning, when it will take less time to heal.

This is beginning to break the stigma associated with mental health conditions. The more individuals share their challenges in an honest and open way, the hope is others will do the same.

I too have been on my own journey of improving my mental health and well-being, and wrote this in a book, **"Say Yes to New Opportunities! Be Motivated to L.E.A.R.N."**

### How Does This Relate to our Journey of Faith?

As individuals we are multi-dimensional. If we start to look after our spiritual wellbeing, it's going to have an impact on other areas of our life. It's like we hold up a mirror and look at the reflection and then decide which other areas need to be improved as well.

There are five areas of our wellbeing. I refer to these as **S.P.I.E.S.** - **S**ocial, **P**hysical, **I**ntellectual, **E**motional and **S**piritual. If even one of them are out of balance it will impact the other areas.

If you were to take a wellbeing audit, which area(s) would you feel you need to improve?

Once you have identified the area(s) what next? Just as growing in your relationship with God, is a journey, looking after these areas too, is a journey.

The way you think is important, at this time. Are you an optimistic or pessimistic person? Is the glass half full or half empty?

What *will* keep you going, when challenges come your way? I would like to say having a positive mindset. As I tell the children in school, "You will make more progress if you have a **Growth Mindset** instead of a **Fixed Mindset**".

As the prodigal son, made his journey back home, there would have been many times when negative words and thoughts would have come into his mind.

"*I am not worthy.*"

"*I am a failure.*"

"*Who would love me?*"

"*I am ...*"

What words come into your mind, when you are feeling low or you know you have messed up your life because of indecisions or decisions you have made? When you have these negative words or thoughts, what can you do?

## The Importance of Affirmations

Before I started my own personal journey of faith, I did not know about the importance of affirmations.

These are sentences you tell yourself which start with the words **I am** ....

I knew words were powerful, but I'm learning how powerful they are, especially when I use affirmations in a positive or negative way. Some call this positive or negative self-talk.

At first, I was encouraged to write ten, different **I am** statements about myself. I found this difficult as I am not used to complimenting myself.

Are you like how I was, or are you able to praise yourself easily?

This would be a good time to take a break and write yourself a list of affirmations. I have given you a few examples below.

1. I am a kind person.
2. I am hardworking.
3. I am loved by my family
4. I am also loved by God.
5. I am blessed and have the favour of God in my life.
6. I am fearfully and wonderfully made, from when I was inside my mother's womb.
7. I am enough.

As you continue with your own list, you will feel your mood change. You cannot still feel low when you are thinking positive thoughts. When you feel low in the future take out your list and read it; as this will lift your mood. Better still, add other affirmations to your list. At the time of writing, I have at least 40 affirmations, that I say to myself on a regular basis. I even have taken a picture of them, on my phone, so I can read them anywhere I am.

## The Importance of Claiming God's Promises

As well as affirmations, it is good to know you can claim the many promises found in God's Word.

Again, I will share six of my favourite promises, from the Bible, but you can add your own.

*1.* **Proverbs 3: 5- 6** *(KJV),* *"Trust in the LORD with all your heart, and lean not on your own understanding; In all your ways acknowledge Him, And He shall direct your paths"*

2. **Philippians 4:6- 7** *(KJV),* *"Be anxious for nothing, but in everything by prayer and supplication, with thanksgiving, let your requests be made known to God; and the peace of God, which surpasses all understanding, will guard your hearts and minds through Christ Jesus,"*

3.  **Philippians 4:19** *(KJV)*, *"And my God shall supply all your needs according to His riches in glory by Christ Jesus.")*.

4.  **Jeremiah 29: 11** *(KJV)* *"For I know the thoughts that I think toward you, says the LORD, thoughts of peace and not of evil, to give you a future and a hope.".*

5.  **John 14: 1-3** *(KJV)*, *"Let not your heart be troubled; you believe in God, believe also in Me. In My Father's house are many mansions; if it were not so, I would have told you. I go to prepare a place for you. And if I go and prepare a place for you, I will come again and receive you to Myself; that where I am, there you may be also."*

6.  **Isaiah 43: 2** *(KJV)*, *"When you pass through the waters, I will be with you; And through the rivers, they shall not overflow you. When you walk through the fire, you shall not be burned, nor shall the flame scorch you."*

These and other Bible promises, I have written on post-it notes and placed in key places in my home so that I can read them as I carry out daily tasks, like brushing my teeth. I would encourage you to do the same.

## The Importance of Singing

Alongside affirmations and Bible promises, another tool which improved my mindset was having a song in my heart. Not just one song but several songs. These songs range from hymns, to praise and worship songs and inspirational songs.

## Protected with God's Armour

In addition to affirming ourselves, claiming the promises found in the Bible, using them as prayers together with singing hymns as well as praise and worship songs to God, we will still need other tools to help us on our journey.

These tools are to help us win our spiritual battle. In **Ephesians 6:10-20**, you are told to put on the full amour of God. This armour protects you from the crown of your head to the sole of your feet. This armour will help you defend yourself when the enemy attacks.

What is in this armour?

1. The belt of truth.
2. The breastplate of righteousness
3. Feet shod with the gospel of peace
4. Shield of faith
5. Helmet of salvation
6. Sword of the Spirit.

As you put on these items, God has promised you He will walk besides you and help you to fight your battles. Your confidence in Him, will improve, as well as your mindset because you are adequately equipped for the journey you are taking. You are now in a much better position to make your way home towards Father God.

**Lessons from the Prodigal Son**

As he made his way home, he rehearsed time and again what he would say to his father.

*"Father, I have sinned against heaven and in your sight, and am no longer worthy to be called your son. Make me like one of your hired servants."* **(Luke 15:21, NASB)**

When the prodigal son arrived home, he started to say what he had rehearsed. He was not able to say anything past "Father" before his father interrupted him by telling the servant to bring his best robe, put a ring on his hand, and sandals on his feet.

The son would have been happy to be a servant, but instead he was reinstated as a son.

You too may have rehearsed the words you want to say to God because of the way you have lived your life. You too may feel you have messed up and He cannot love you. When we address our "Father", God responds.

But just as the father did for the prodigal son, God is going to do the same for you. He will interrupt those negative thought. He will take them off and reset and renew your mind.

God will take off your outer garment and give you His best robe, a robe of righteousness. He will also give you a crown for your head, and a mansion as a new home.

If the prodigal son had stayed where he was, look at the blessings he would have missed out of. If you stay where you are, and do not start, or continue your journey of faith, look at what blessings you too would be missing.

The changes in your life, will not start when you get the gifts in heaven of a robe of righteousness, a crown and a mansion. NO! The blessings start here on earth. The journey to your eternal home, begins with how you live your life here on earth - now!

**God's Blessings on Earth**

On earth you will start to develop your character, by changing your mindset. Before long the fruit of the Spirit as shown in **Galatians 5:22-23** will be seen in your life. "Love, joy, peace, longsuffering, kindness, goodness, faithfulness, gentleness and self-control."

As others see the change, you will become a magnet. People will become attracted to the new you and will want to know what has changed in your life. You are then able to share with them the journey of faith you have been on, and this is an ideal time to encourage them to also start or continue their own journey of faith. This is what it means to be a disciple of Jesus. This is how you become a good witness, by sharing your own personal testimony.

Have you now taken the first four steps in this journey of faith?

1. Have you made the decision to have a deeper relationship with God?
2. Have you shared this decision with others in a public way?
3. Are you now able to be real with your emotions?
4. Have you adopted a positive mindset?

If so, you are now ready to take the fifth step. You are ready to set yourself goals to work towards being successful.

Even if you have not made these decisions, you will still find value in continuing to read this book on your journey.

# CHAPTER 5

## *Success! What Does This Word Mean to You?*

When you hear the word **success** what picture comes into your mind?

Someone who has a lot of money and has financial freedom?

Someone who is a world leader?

Someone who is a celebrity?

In the story of the prodigal son, I would say the end part of his story made him successful. He was welcomed back into the family home and his status was reinstated. This was much more than he expected when he started his journey home.

When the father pleaded and encouraged the eldest son to come into the celebration, he said,

*"Son, you are always with me, and all that I have is yours. It was right that we should make merry and be glad, for your brother was dead and is alive again, and was lost and is found."*

From this story, what makes someone successful?

I would like to say a person who is surrounded by people who loves them, and they are doing a role they like, willingly can be seen to be successful. If that role is impacting the lives of others in a positive way, then that will make them even more successful, as the focus is on '**we**' and not '**me**.' They have become empowered, to bring out their greatness from within. God wants to empower you.

At the start of this book, I raised three important questions.

1. **How important is God in your life?**
2. **Do you have a personal relationship with God?**
3. **Where are you planning to spend eternity?**

If someone was to now ask you the question, "**How important is God in your life?**" How would you respond?

On the scale of **0 to 10** what number would you now give your relationship with Him? Has it changed from the number you gave yourself when you first started to read this book? If yes, what has caused the number to increase or decrease?

You may be surprised I have said the number may decrease. I fully believe in all sincerity when you answered the question the first time, you thought your relationship with God was a 9 or 10, but with new insight from reading the first four chapters of this book, you may now want to reduce your number.

This is a good sign, and you need to be commended, if this is you.

### Has Your relationship With God Changed?

What image of God do you now have? As a loving Father, who is waiting for you with open arms or someone who is waiting to punish you if you slip up?

If you were to paint a picture of Him on a canvas what would He look like? What traits would you put on the picture? Open arms or closed arms? Running or standing still? A smile on His face or a frown? Your image of God will determine your answer to the final question.

*"Where are you planning to spend eternity?"*

This is a critical question; one many do not take time to think about.

**You decide where your final destination is going to be from the relationship you have with God on earth.**

Are you going to be like the younger son who, realised that although he had made many big plans, he made many big mistakes in his life? Yet, his Father had forgiven him and had welcomed him home to a celebration? Or, on the other hand, are you going to be like the eldest son who refused to go into the celebration? His father could encourage him, but would not force him to go somewhere he would not be happy.

God is pleading with each one of His children to come to the celebration He has prepared for us in heaven, too. When Jesus comes back to take us home, some will accept the invitation to go home with Him, but many will reject the invitation. He will not force us, He will not force you, to attend the celebration.

I hope by now you have made the decision to attend the celebration, and want to take the next step. This involves you sharing your journey with others. Just as Jesus sent out the 12 or 70 to prepare the way for Him and His ministry, He is sending you out to share your experiences with others to prepare them for His Second Coming.

**The Importance of Goal Setting**

If you have made the decision to go and share your journey with others, to be successful, it is good to have a plan.

This next step will put all that you have learnt together. What have been your areas of strength and your areas of development? For your areas of strength what strategies do you need to put into place to maintain them? For your areas of development, what steps do you need to put into place, to improve them?

When setting goals, it's always advised to make them **SMART** goals.

These are **S**pecific, **M**easurable, **A**chievable, **R**ealistic and **T**ime related.

Set yourself two or three goals you can work towards to improve your ability to share your new experiences with others.

## Putting it All Together

You have now completed five steps in your journey of faith and reached the halfway point. I hope by now you have made a commitment to continue deepening your relationship with God and are continuing to read not out of curiosity, but to grow your faith.

1. Have you made the decision to have a deeper relationship with God?
2. Have you shared this decision with others in a public way?
3. Are you real with your emotions?
4. Have you adopted a positive mindset?

5. Have you set yourself goals to be more successful in your journey?

If you have answered yes to these questions, you are now ready to move onto the next phase of your journey of faith, sharing what you have learnt with others.

In this phase you will learn about the importance of '**we**' and not '**me**', in your relationships with others. You will see the benefits of being in a **TEAM** and not an 'I'.

The word **TEAM** means **T**ogether **E**veryone **A**chieves **M**ore!

# CHAPTER 6

## *Am I An Effective Listener?*

In the first half of the book we looked at this journey of faith through the eyes of the Prodigal son. He was in a loving home, living with his brother and father and servants. In many biblical stories the names of women are not mentioned unless their input was very significant in the story; so, we do not know if his mother was with him as well. Despite having all he needed at home, this son was not happy and wanted to leave home and go and discover life for himself. He wanted to leave his father's presence. We are told in **Luke 15:13**,

> *"And not many days after, the younger son gathered all together, journeyed to a far country, and there wasted his possessions with prodigal living."*

**What Were the Steps This Son Took?**

1. He had a conversation with his father.
2. The father listened and gave him his portion of goods.

3.  He stayed at home for a few days, and did not change his mind. I am sure during those few days the father would have pleaded with him to stay.

4.  He left home and journeyed to a far country.

5.  He wasted his possessions with prodigal living.

6.  When he had spent everything, a famine came in the land.

7.  He found himself in a position of want and nobody was there for him.

8.  He went and worked for a citizen of the country. He sent him to his field to feed swine. (For a Jewish son, this was one of the worst jobs he would want to do).

9.  He was so hungry he would have eaten the food he was feeding the pigs, because no one gave him anything to eat.

10. **Then**, he came to himself and realised his servants at home were being treated better than he was now, in this far country.

In the biblical account, at each stage of his journey his actions took him further and further away from the life he knew at home. But one day we are told, "*He came to himself* " (**Luke 15:17**).

As he sat looking after the swine, he would have had a lot of time to think and reflect on his life. Distractions would have been few. He would have had a lot of time to reflect on his life and the effects of the choices he had taken which now resulted in him looking after swine, and hungry. He knew his actions, not only affected him, but also his family. His actions had caused his father great pain.

What about you? Are you sat at home with a lot of time to think and reflect on your life? Are distractions few? Do you have time to reflect on your life and the effects of the choices you have taken? Are you pained by yours or others decisions? Are you in a lot of pain due to the actions that have impacted your choices?

You do not need to remain there, in your thoughts. Just like with the prodigal son, you can make the decision to go back home, to live your life in a renewed way.

## The Importance of our Thoughts

Do you have conversations with yourself? When you have these conversations, they take place in your thoughts and mind.

The prodigal son, also would have had conversations with himself.

Our thoughts originate in our head.

In the silence all around him, the prodigal son would have had a long time to listen to his thoughts. He probably had not really listened to them for years.

He would have been distracted by other things happening in his life.

**What about you?**

During the time of lockdown and social isolation, you too may have had a lot of silence all around you.

Have you been able to have a long time to listen to your thoughts? You probably have not listened to them for years, as you were so busy on the treadmill. The hamster wheel of life, may have just been going round and round, without a clear end. Now with many distractions removed, have you had time to really listen to yourself and your inner voice.

I'm not talking here about the shallow listening you do, the fleeting thoughts, no I am talking about the deep listening you do when you are all alone with no distraction. The times when you are still, and it is only you and God who hears them. The times when He has your full attention. This was one of those times, for this prodigal son.

This may also be one of those times for you.

## Personal Application

When was the last time you had a deep conversation with God? A conversation where it was just the two of you alone for at least an hour, but preferably half a day. Time when the two of you communicated together, honestly.

This time will give you the opportunity to pour out your heart to Him about all of the things, which you are grateful for in life, but also the areas you need His help and direction with. In these moments He will listen to you and He wants you to listen to Him. He wants to have a dialogue and not a monologue with you.

It's good when you have these conversations to take a notebook, or some other means to record the points discussed, including the actions taken or to be taken. It will make the time even more special. Days, weeks, months, or even years later you'll be able to regularly review and see the significance of these conversations. You will be able to see God's hand at work, behind the scenes in answers to your many conversations called prayers.

For many the thought of spending half a day in God's presence, can feel quiet daunting, just you and Him alone, especially if you are used to only praying for 2 or 3 minutes, at the start and end of each day or none at all!

Let's be honest, could you develop any relationship with anyone that way? No!

This is why in **Chapter 4**, I shared ways to develop this relationship between you and God, to spend quality time with Him. These strategies are: -

1.   Have a positive image of who God is.  He is your loving Father who wants to have a relationship with you. He wants to have a dialogue not a monologue.

2.   Develop a positive image of yourself, with the use of affirmations. You need to see yourself through the eyes of God. You are His son or daughter, who He wants to get to know intimately and He wants you to get to know Him intimately too.

3.   To develop this relationship, He has given you promises found in His Word, called the Bible, for you to claim for yourself, and then apply them to your life. In His Word, are many stories of individuals who have had challenges in their life and the impact of the decisions and choices they made. They are recorded to encourage you, to keep you walking in your journey of faith.

4.   Have a song or several songs in your heart, which will lift you into His presence. God's presence is nearer to us when we give Him praise and worship, for who He is, not for what He does; there is a big difference.

As you apply these four strategies daily in your life, you will see growth in your relationship with God. You will find you want to listen to His voice more and more. You will want to allow Him to work collaboratively with you along your faith journey. Before long, you'll be longing for the times you can spend half a day in His presence!

For the second half of this book, we are going to look at two individuals who took a journey of faith. We find these individuals in the Old Testament, and their stories are written in the book that shares my name, Ruth. You will discover, as you continue reading, there are many similarities between the story of the prodigal son and the story of Ruth and Naomi.

**Elimelech's Family Moves to Moab**.

In **Ruth 1:1** we are introduced to the family of Elimelech. He was the father of two sons, Mahlon and Chilion. He was married to Naomi. He lived in Bethlehem with his family. A famine came, and as a result, he moved his family to a distant country, Moab.

Like the prodigal son, they would have waited a few days before taking this journey, once the decision was made. They would have said their goodbyes to family and friends, and made the necessary arrangements for their property, before setting off.

As they walked, conversations would have continued. Each step of the journey they would have been communicating and listening to each other.

The family eventually arrived in Moab and made arrangements to have a new home there. After some time Elimelech died. Naomi was left a widow, needing to be cared for by her sons, who took wives from the women of Moab, Orpah and Ruth. We are told they lived together for about ten years and then Mahlon and Chilion also died.

## Naomi Returns to Bethlehem

We are not told how, but Naomi received the message there was bread back in Bethlehem, because the LORD had visited His people and ended the famine, so she made the decision to return home, alone.

She had arrived in Moab, full, and now was going to return empty. She arrived happy and now was going to return sad. She arrived in Moab looking forward to having a future. She was going home to Bethlehem, but despondent.

As was the custom of the day, when you became a widow, Naomi shared with her daughter in laws her plans, to return home to Bethlehem, and encouraged them to go back home to their families, She reminded them their family would take care of them. *"I am not in a position to look after you now, and if I was to have any other children, are you prepared to wait until they are old?"* Naomi said to them.

Naomi was enquiring from them, if they would be prepared to wait at least 20 years, before they would be able to marry again; if Naomi was able to have another husband, and be able to have sons, which she could not guarantee.

Orpah, reflected on her options and with tears in her eyes, she kissed Naomi, for one last time and made the decision to return home.

Ruth on the other hand, made a bold decision. She said to Naomi, *"I am not going to let you take this journey to Bethlehem alone. I am going to go with you. I am going to take this journey of faith with you. I am going to make this promise to you and I want you to listen carefully."* The words of this promise are found in **Ruth 1:16-17, (NKJ)**

*"Entreat me not to leave you, Or to turn back from following after you. For wherever you go, I will go. And wherever you lodge, I will lodge. Your people shall be my people, And your God, my God. Where you die, I will die, And there will I be buried. The LORD does so to me, and more also, If anything but death parts you and me."*

Naomi listened to Ruth, and together they made the journey from Moab to Bethlehem. It would not have been an easy journey, two women alone, but I believe God was with them. I believe God sent His angels to protect them.

As we read in **Psalms 34:7,** *"For the angel of the LORD is a guard; He surrounds and defends all who fear Him."*

When I leave home and go on a journey I too pray and ask the angel of the Lord to guard me, and protect all who are with me from any harm, and bring us back home safely.

We do not know how long the journey took, but when Ruth and Naomi arrived home it was the beginning of the barley harvest.

Naomi would have been able to say, "I **AM HOME AT LAST!**"

## How Does This Relate to Our Journey of Faith?

In life we face so many challenges and as a result we have to make decisions which could literally disrupt the lives of all members of our families. When Elimelech went to Moab, I am sure he thought he was going there for a short period of time, to keep his family safe. Things did not work out as planned, because we are told he died. After the period of mourning passed, and with her sons at an age to marry, they took wives from Moab.

The people of Moab, followed different customs and beliefs and in an ideal situation, they would not have taken wives from Moab, but would have done as Abraham did for Isaac, after Sarah, his wife, died. They would have made arrangements to get wives from amongst their own people or clan. (**Genesis 24:1-27**). However, this option was not available.

The sons married, but remained childless. After a period of time, we are told the sons died too.

Looking at this story through the eyes of Naomi, it appeared to be a series of doors of opportunities opening and closing. Her life events were such that when each door closed, she was left in even greater pain than when the previous door closed.

Can you relate to this? Doors keep opening and closing on you. As each door closes you are left in greater pain. So much pain, you are not able to cry any more. So much pain you feel your heart will break. So much pain you feel numb. So much pain you do not want to eat. So much pain that like Elijah, you ask God to let you die (**1Kings 19:1-14**). When you may get pain this deep, you can feel as if God has rejected you also. You may feel all alone and abandoned!

But God was with Naomi all along. He was with her, and her family, when they moved to Moab. He was with her, when Ruth became her daughter-in- law. He was with them as they took this journey back to Bethlehem. He was with them each step of the way.

When things became too much for them, He carried them safely in His arms. As He walked beside them or carried them, He was listening effectively to their prayers. God is listening effectively to your prayers too. Be encouraged to take the next step, in your journey of faith. Father God is there with you each step you take!

**HE HAS NOT ABANDONED YOU!**

# CHAPTER 7

## *Am I Engaged?*

Ruth and Naomi arrived back in Bethlehem and made their way to Naomi's home; the one she had left behind. As Naomi reflected on the journey of her life since her family made the decision to travel to Moab, so many emotions overwhelmed her. As she entered through the door of the home, she had left, she thought of others who had remained.

*"Would things have been different if we too had remained?"*

*"Would I still have my husband and sons?"*

Just, as in the past, Ruth was there to support her mother-in-law and encouraged her. She reminded her of the promise she made, *"I'll stay by your side."*

### Ruth Becomes Engaged in Work

Ruth and Naomi needed food to eat, and so as the custom was, Ruth went to gather grain in a barley field. She went into the field of Boaz, a relative of Naomi's husband, a man of great wealth. As Ruth left home in the morning, she said to Naomi,

83

*"Let me go out into the harvest fields to pick up the stalks of grain left behind by anyone who is kind enough to let me do it,"* **Ruth 2:2.**

*"Each day as Boaz arrived from Bethlehem and greeted the harvesters. "The LORD be with you!" he said. "The LORD bless you!" the harvesters replied,"* **Ruth 2:4.**

Boaz was observant and he noticed a new reaper. She looked different than the other reapers. She stood out from the crowd. He asked who she was. He was told her name was Ruth, a Moabite woman, who had returned with Naomi, from the country of Moab. When Boaz, found out who she was, he gave strict instructions about how to treat her to the servant who was in charge of the reapers. He put in place things to provide for her needs as she worked, and also for her protection.

God had answered the prayer Ruth had shared with Naomi in the morning. She had found favour in the eyes of Boaz. As she continued to work in the field, he also encouraged her to come and have a meal with him and the other reapers.

When she returned home with the barley grain she had gathered, Naomi knew she had gathered much more than expected and had gained a blessing from God. As Ruth shared her account of what had taken place, Naomi knew God had not left her and was still providing for her needs. Naomi replied in **Ruth 2:20b,**

*"May the LORD bless him! He is showing his kindness to us as well as to your dead husband."*

Naomi then gave Ruth instructions as to how to continue to find favour with Boaz as she gleaned in his field, and how to keep herself safe. Ruth went out each day and gleaned until the end of the barley harvest, as instructed.

## How Does This Relate to Your Journey of Faith?

When Ruth made the decision to leave Moab and return to Bethlehem with Naomi, she was turning her back on a life of certainty to one of uncertainty. She was turning away from a faith she had grown up with, to embrace a new faith. She was turning her back on her family and embracing a new family. It would have been easy for her to stay in Moab, but something within her was moving her forward in a new direction. What was moving her forward was the seed of faith which was planted within her. This seed had now started to grow and produced roots.

As she spent time with Naomi, she came to love not just her mother-in-law, but also her God. This was why she was prepared to leave Moab; she wanted to learn more about this God.

You too may have seen in others the impact of having a relationship with God has in their life. You may wish to have similar experiences, but you are worried about how it will change your life. Whether you have attended church for years, even decades, or not, deep down you know there is something missing. That drive to know something better is what faith is about. This is what the journey of faith is about. You take the initial step, but the more you travel, you realise there is still more to learn. Much more!

When Ruth left home in the morning to go and glean, she did not know what to do. She observed and copied. Eventually she was noticed and she was asked to join the group, to take part in their activities. As part of the group she was taught how to glean, and soon she was accepted as a member of the community. If Ruth, did not decide to engage in the process, things would have been so different for her.

We probably would never have heard about her story, and she would never have had a book in the Bible written about her journey of faith. Remember women were not mentioned in Bible stories unless their impact was significant. Not only is she mentioned, she has a book named after her!

You may be at the start of your journey of faith. You may or may not have started attending a place of worship, or you may or may not have started to listen to a church service online.

Most places of worship should have someone to look after new interests and visitors. As you attend the service or watch online, you will just copy what you're seeing happening around you. The more you decide to engage, the more you will discover a growing interest to attend the same meeting. From first-hand experience, the more you engage, the better your experience will be.

You may have attended a place of worship for a long time. If this is you, be like the servant and look out for new people arriving, and welcome them into your group. Sit with them and explain what is happening in each part of the meeting. They will appreciate the guidance given to them.

At this moment, when writing, we are not able to meet in our places of worship, but having to listen online. For many online services, you may invite someone to join you for the service. When you have finished listening to the service together, don't forget to give your guest a call to see if they have any questions.

In the week ahead, phone them and continue to develop this new phase of your relationship. As you build this relationship with them you can help them move from spectator to participant especially if you are able to encourage your guest to join in with any discussions you may be having as part of your services.

## The Importance of Perseverance

When Naomi made the decision to return home, she said in **Ruth 1: 20,**

*"Don't call me Naomi. Instead, call me Mara, for the Almighty has made life very bitter for me."*

Now in **Ruth 2:20,** she is saying,

*"May the LORD bless him! He is showing his kindness to us as well as to your dead husband."*

Naomi had realised that although her circumstances had changed, God had not changed. He was still being faithful and looking after her needs and that of Ruth. She was able to see the hand of God at work in the events taking place in their lives.

Are you facing challenges in your life, so you too want to use the name Mara instead of your own?

Have you started a project full of ideas and resources which then has been taken away and you are left feeling empty?

Do you feel as if the Almighty has afflicted you?

Have you experienced a great loss which is leaving you feeling empty inside? Let's look at why Naomi was feeling this way.

## What Were the Steps Naomi and her Family Took?

1.  She had a conversation with her husband Elimelech and they made the decision to leave Bethlehem to go to Moab.

2.  They shared this news with their sons Mahlon and Chilion.

3.  They stayed at home for a few days and made arrangements with other family members to look after their property whilst they were away.

4.  They left their home in Bethlehem and journey to a far country, Moab.

5.  Whilst there Elimelech died and Naomi becomes a widow, who needed to be cared for by her sons.

6.  Her sons took wives of the women of Moab, Orpah and Ruth.

7.  Mahlon and Chilion died, so now there were three widows, not just one.

8.  Naomi decided she was going to return home to Bethlehem and encouraged Orpah and Ruth to return home to their families.

9. Orpah decided to go back home, but Ruth made a promise to Naomi she would go back to Bethlehem with her.

10. Naomi returned home to Bethlehem with Ruth, feeling rejected and forsaken by God. She said, she had left full, but was returning empty.

## What Journey Have You Taken?

If you were to describe your journey of faith so far in 10 steps what would they be? What was your starting point? It is usually an event or decision you have taken that moves you from where you are to a new place? How do you feel about the journey of faith you have taken so far?

Can you see light at the end of the tunnel or is there still darkness?

Are you taking the journey alone, as with the prodigal son, or with others, as with Naomi and her family?

What changes have taken place along the way, if any?

What further decisions have you taken and what has been the impact?

**Now would be a good time to stop reading, and reflect on your answers to the questions above.**

## What Lessons Have You Learnt?

Did you find your time of reflection useful?

Both the prodigal son and Naomi set off from their homes.

In both of their stories there was a famine, and they needed the support of others to survive.

Both the prodigal son and Naomi, after a period of time, made the decision to return home.

Both were greeted by the community they had left behind upon their return.

Both were able to say, "I am home at last!"

## A Time of Reflection

In your journey of faith, challenges will happen. Things will not go as planned. It can leave you feeling isolated, and hurt and you may feel God has abandoned you also. But as He was there with the prodigal son, and was there with Naomi, He is there with you, right by your side.

Both were able to recognise the blessings of God. The prodigal son was accepted back into his family and community and Naomi was able to see through the action of Boaz. She and Ruth had been accepted back into the community she had left behind, when her family went to Moab.

The acceptance into their respective communities was a direct result of their engagement with others. I hope you too will make the decision to first spend quality time in personal devotion with God, and then spend time with others, contributing your skills and talents to building up a local community.

You will find the more time you engage with others your relationship with both God and others will become more intimate. As you are spending more time thinking about the needs of others, it will help you to develop a more positive mindset and improve your self-worth.

# CHAPTER 8

## *Do I Have the Right Attitude?*

With the favour Boaz showed Ruth, and the fact he was a relative of her late husband Elimelech, Naomi wondered if he could be the answer to their prayers.

Would he be the one to restore dignity to their family?

Would he be the one to provide for their needs, not just whilst the barley harvest was being gathered, but long- term.

Naomi, knowing she was advancing in years, wanted to ensure she provided for Ruth's security. She also knew it would have to be someone special who would take her as his wife, because she was a Moabite.

### Naomi's Plan

Naomi knew the customs of her village and what would take place in the evening, at the celebration for the end of the harvest. She told Ruth to go and wash herself, anoint herself with sweet smelling perfume and put on her best clothes. Her time of mourning the loss of her husband would now come to an end. She was then to go down to the threshing floor and not let Boaz see her until he had finished eating and drinking. When he went to lie down, Ruth should notice the place where he was lying down and she should go and uncover his feet and lie down. She was told Boaz would tell her what to do next. What was Ruth's response to the instructions given to her from Naomi? She replied, *"All that you say to me I will do."* [paraphrased]

Ruth did not understand all of the things she was being told, but because she trusted Naomi, she adopted the right attitude.

She did not ask like so many people would today, *"Why?"*

For many people, everything must have an explanation and when you cannot answer their why, they get upset. They do not understand in life some instructions need to be followed, without a detailed explanation. This is what faith is about; following instructions without always knowing what the final outcome would be.

### How Does This Relate to Our Journey of Faith?

This book is a called "Home at Last" and the key text is found in *Joshua 1:9,*

*"This is my command—be strong and courageous! Do not be afraid or discouraged. For the LORD your God is with you wherever you go."*

When Joshua set off on the journey to cross over the River Jordan, he didn't know what challenges he would face, but he knew he could trust God. He knew he could be strong and courageous. He didn't need to be afraid or discouraged, because he knew the Lord his God was with him, wherever he went.

Years before, in Joshua's journey of faith, when the Israelites started to occupy Canaan, he would have met Rahab. The spies who hid on her roof would have told him about the promise they had given to her. All those who would be found in her home, would be protected, when the city of Jericho would be finally destroyed.

Now Naomi, is having a conversation with Ruth, about Boaz, who is the son of Rahab. God truly is a Waymaker!

We are reminded in **Hebrews 11:1 (NKJ),** *"Now faith is the substance of things hoped for, and the evidence of things not seen."*

Faith is the substance of things hoped for. Faith is based on hope.

When Naomi told Ruth her plan, she was hoping it would be successful.

When the prodigal son started his journey back home, he was hoping his father would allow him to become a servant.

What are you hoping for in your personal life?

What are you hoping for in your professional life?

What are you hoping for in your family?

What are you hoping for in your spiritual life?

When we have hope we expect something to happen. It may take a short time to happen, or a much longer period of time.

We can become despondent when things we hope for are delayed. If your waiting is too long, will you turn back? Will you abandon your journey? What if you had stayed just a little while longer, will you have gotten what they had hoped for?

Let's go back to the story of Abraham. We know God made a covenant to Him that He would be the father of nations. The promise was not fulfilled in his lifetime, but several generations later.

There are times when our hopes are not in line with God's plan for our life. Like Abraham and the prodigal son we have looked at in this book, He gives us free choice to make decisions.

Would you expect Him to act any other way?

## Where is Your Hope?

As I am finalising this book, it is November 2020. The world is still in the middle of the pandemic, the second wave, and many are losing hope. All around them they can see pain, and the loss of loved ones, and lost dreams.

Since November 2019, I have lost nine significant members of my extended family and friends, not COVID-19 related, and it was not easy to have to lay them to rest knowing we will not be able to see each other again, or speak again on the phone. Some of my family lived in different countries around the world, so we could not attend their funerals, as there were no flights abroad.

Sad though the occasions have been, at the back of our minds, we have been comforted with the words found in **1 Corinthians 15:51,**

*"But let me reveal to you a wonderful secret. We will not all die, but we will all be transformed!"*

As we have attended the funeral services or watched online, we were comforted with the hope we will be reunited when Jesus returns never to be parted again. When He comes back, some will still be alive to see Him whilst others will rise from their graves. But here is the good news, WE WILL all be transformed.

I do not know if you too are grieving the loss of loved ones, but be encouraged, there is a time coming, when you and I will be reunited with our loved ones, never to part from them again, following the Second Coming of Jesus, as **KING OF KINGS AND LORD OF LORDS**.

We can be confident to know that the world will not end due to a climate change catastrophe, or a pandemic. We know the world will end, as the Bible states, with the Second Coming of Jesus. Be comforted to know God is still in control of this earth, and nothing takes Him by surprise.

**Be Transformed!**

In order for us to be transformed, an intimate relationship with God is important before Jesus comes the Second time, whilst we are here on earth. We will not change our character when we get to heaven, just our body!

The Bible tells us in **2 Peter 1:5- 8** how to develop this character.

*"In view of all this, make every effort to respond to God's promises. Supplement your faith with a generous provision of moral excellence, and moral excellence with knowledge, and knowledge with self-control, and self-control with patient*

*endurance, and patient endurance with godliness, and godliness with brotherly affection, and brotherly affection with love for everyone. The more you grow like this, the more productive and useful you will be in your knowledge of our Lord Jesus Christ."*

As you travel along on your own personal journey of faith, God will ask you to do things which you may not always understand, but because of your relationship with Him, you too should respond like Ruth, "**All you say to me I will do!**"

As you daily make this declaration and obey His voice, your life will be transformed. At first you will have your own inward personal revival. Later changes will take place which will be observed by others. Your habits will change. Your character will change.

As others observe your life, they will see the fruit of the Spirit as described in **Galatians 5:22- 23,** being lived in practical ways.

*"But the Holy Spirit produces this kind of fruit in our lives:love,joy,peace, patience, kindness,goodness, faithfulness, gentleness, and self-control. There is no law against these things!"*

Love is the first part of the fruit, and we can see it was love which drove Ruth, Naomi and Boaz to act as they did. What action is love driving you to do?

### Boaz's Respond to Ruth

Ruth went to the celebration and did all Naomi told her to do. At midnight Boaz turned in his sleep, and was startled to see a woman lying at his feet. He asked, "Who are you?"

"*I am your servant Ruth,*" she replied. "*Spread the corner of your covering over me, for you are my family redeemer.*"

"*The* LORD *bless you, my daughter!*" Boaz exclaimed. "*You are showing even more family loyalty now than you did before, for you have not gone after a younger man, whether rich or poor,*" (**Ruth 3:9,10**).

He reassured her in the morning he would perform the duty of the close relative on her behalf. He reminded her there was a closer relative, but if he decided not to carry out his duty, he, Boaz would be true to his word. He told her to stay where she was for the night and in the morning return home to Naomi. She was not to tell anyone she has spent the night on the threshing floor.

In the morning, Boaz used the shawl which covered her during the night, to put in six ephahs (scoops) of barley in, and said she should not return to Naomi empty-handed. He reassured her by the end of the day, she would have an answer to her request. Ruth's actions as directed by Naomi, symbolised a request. The request was, *"Will you take your maidservant under your wing for you are a close relative?"* Ruth returned home and told Naomi all that had taken place.

What would have happened if Ruth had not followed Naomi's instructions exactly as she told her to do? Ruth took a great risk, but her courage was rewarded as we will read about in the next chapter.

Going on your journey of faith will require you also to take risks and be courageous; just like Joshua and Ruth were!

# CHAPTER 9

## *The Importance Of Reflection Time*

Boaz was true to his word. We read in **Ruth Chapter 4**, that same morning he went to the gate where the men met to conduct business and sat down. As he waited the man who was the closest relative to Naomi came by. He asked him to sit down with him. Boaz also called ten men who were elders of the city, and asked them to sit down too.

Boaz then put his case to all of the men assembled. He explained Naomi was back from Moab and had sold a piece of land which belonged to their brother Elimelech. He told the closer relative he should buy it back and redeem it for the family.

The close relative agreed to buy it back, however, he changed his mind when he realised, he would have to marry Ruth and continue Elimelech's name and his inheritance. This was too great a price for him to pay! He wanted his own family line, not that of his relative Elimelech.

This was the response Boaz was expecting. The relative took off his sandal and told Boaz, "*Buy it for yourself.*"

Boaz agreed to the sale and said to the men assembled, "*This day I have brought all that was Elimelech's, and all that was Chilion's and Mahlon's from the hand of Naomi. I am also taking Ruth, who was the wife of Mahlon as my wife, so I can restore the name of the deceased to his inheritance, so his name will not be cut off from his brothers or from the gate of his birthplace. The elders then gave him a special blessing,*

"***May the LORD make Ruth, who is coming into your home like Rachel and Leah, the two who built the household of Israel*** *May you achieve wealth and power in Ephrathah and become famous in Bethlehem. Further, may your house be like the house of Perez whom Tamar bore to Judah, because of the offspring which the LORD will give you by this young woman.*" (***Ruth 4:11,12 AMP***).

They blessed his household and any offspring which the LORD will give to Ruth.

Boaz had gone to the gate to meet the elders to fulfil the proceedings required to take Ruth as his wife and to be able to look after Naomi. He was not obliged to do this, as it was someone else's responsibility. They relinquished their responsibility as they felt it was too much to have to look after Ruth and Naomi. Boaz cared and as a result he ended up with so much more. He ended up with blessings being said for his immediate family and generations to come.

### The Meeting of the Elders

As Boaz sat in the meeting with the elders of the city, he was able to reflect on the relationship of Elimelech and his family before he went to Moab. Elimelech was probably one of the elders who would have been consulted about important decisions which needed to be made.

Now everyone had an opportunity to look after his family in his absence. They knew he would like his name to be preserved, because ancestral lineage was important. They also knew one day an important member of the family would be born though this lineage, who would be called The Redeemer or Messiah.

When the children of Israel were given the Promised Land as their inheritance, Moses gave clear instructions to Joshua, about how they were to conduct their business affairs to ensure widows where taken care of, and these practices were the ones being used by Boaz and the elders as they sat in the meeting, that morning.

As the elders also reflected about their past, they remembered the names of women of influence, Rachel, Leah and also Tamar who was the mother of Perez. Rachel and Leah were two of the wives of Jacob. He had 12 sons including Joseph whose mother was Rachel and Judah whose mother was

Leah. After a night of wrestling with God, Jacob's name was changed to Israel.

Perez was the son of Judah and Tamar, and he had a twin brother called Zerah. The elders knew God had blessed Rachel, Leah and their children, and they wanted a similar blessing for Boaz and Ruth.


## Why is Reflecting on Our Past a Good Thing to do?

When Boaz and the elders reflected on their history and heritage, they were able to see how God had preserved the family despite the challenges they had been through.

Abraham had a son named Isaac. He had twin boys named Jacob and Esau. Jacob, had 12 sons by 4 different women, and as you can imagine there was rivalry between the sons. Out of the four 'wives' Jacob loved Rachel the most. When he eventually had a son by her, Joseph, he treated him more favourable than his brothers. He even gave Joseph a coat of many colours. This angered his brothers even more. We are told they hated Joseph. You can read the full story in **Genesis 37.**

Joseph had several dreams, in which he would be a great leader and his brothers and parents would bow down to him. This made the brother dislike him and they were jealous of him.

Fast forward the story. Jacob sends Joseph to go and see how his brothers and the flocks were getting on.

When they see him coming, they decide to kill him, and would tell their father that he was killed by wild animals. Instead they put him into a deep pit. As the brothers were sitting down to eat, they saw some Ishmaelite traders and decided to sell their brother instead. Joseph was then sold as a slave and taken to Egypt.

If Joseph was not sold as a slave and taken to Egypt he would not have been in the right place and position to save his father and the families of his brothers, when they were facing a famine back home. Once again, we read of another story when a famine caused a family to move location and the blessings which took place, due to a journey of faith.

70 members of Joseph's family went to live in Egypt, when the famine occurred. When the Passover took place, 430 years later, which we read about in the introduction, 600,000 men as well as women and children, left Egypt's to go on their journey to Canaan, the Promised Land. No wonder they left as a nation! This was a fulfilment of the covenant God had made to Abraham!

When you look at events which have happened to you in the past, could God be using them to get you to where he needs you to be, so you are able to be more effective, than if you had remained in your old place?

I am beginning to understand, at a deeper level, the text found in **Romans 8:28**, (NKJ),

*"And we know that all things work together for good to those who love God, to those who are the called according to **His** purpose."*

I have been encouraged, as I'm writing this book, to reflect at a deeper level. It is amazing to see how God worked in the lives of individuals in the Bible. He is now using my own life , to encourage you not to give up when challenges come your way. There is strength that comes from getting back up, and not staying down, when we get knocked off our feet.

You may be in the midst of a famine, but be encouraged not to give up!

You may be in the midst of a storm, but be encouraged not to give up!

You may be in the midst of conflict, but be encouraged not to give up!

You may be in the midst of ill health, but be encouraged not to give up!

You may be in the midst of broken promises and dreams, but be encouraged not to give up!

You may be in the midst of grief, but be encouraged not to give up!

You may be in the midst of a pandemic, but be encouraged not to give up!

## DON'T GIVE IN AND DON'T GIVE UP!

When challenges come your way and you face some low times in your life, you may have questioned God and asked Him, "Why?"

You may even go as far as feeling angry with what you are going through. There are three types of anger which individuals may use to react to a situation which makes them feel angry. These are called Passive Aggression, Open Aggression and Assertive Anger.

In passive aggression, you give the person who has hurt you the silent treatment. You pretend everything is fine, when it is not. This type of anger is the most dangerous, as it brews below the surface, and when it explodes, unexpectedly, it can do more damage, than many would expect, especially in relationships.

Open aggression is the one we most know. This is when we say, someone has a short fuse. These individuals shout loudly, fight, bully others, hit walls or punch bags, or use other types of physical or emotional force. These individuals need you to know they are in control. With them, as quickly as the matter arises, a solution of one form or another, is put into place, no matter what the long-term consequences will be, and who they hurt in the process.

In assertive anger, the healthy way to deal with anger, you think before you speak. You think about the needs and welfare of the other person involved in the dispute before you act. You are in control and confident. You take time to listen to the other party, and let them feel in control.

I shared earlier in chapter three; God wants you to be real about your emotions. When you reflected on your past, you may have had a lot of emotions to cope with. When you are going through your reflective mode, it is good to have others around who will support you and allow you to be totally honest about how you are feeling, because long term it will be good for your wellbeing.

Also, as you reflect on your past, you will be able to see how the hand of God has worked in good ways in your life. You will be able to see how He was guiding and directing you all along. You will be able to see He was with you as you walked this faith journey, at the mountains, and down into the valleys.

Be encouraged, however long your journey has taken. The Children of Israel's journey took 40 years!

It too may have taken you decades, even 40 years or longer to fulfil your journey of faith.

## How Does This Relate to my Journey of Faith?

As I was writing these last few paragraphs it has made me reflect on my own life and experiences whilst writing this book. The original version of this book was the quickest book I have written and typed from conception to first draft manuscript. It took just over 48 hours, to write 15,000 words and 52 pages.

I had travelled from London to Oldham, following the death of a family friend, and attending their funeral, I wanted to have some quiet time alone. I did not have the intention to write a new book.

Now we are in the middle of a pandemic. I did not have the intention of adapting the book, sharing things which have happened in my life this year, and around the world. As you can see, once more I am being obedient, and sharing these words of hope Father God has given to me, with you, so you too can be courageous like Joshua, the prodigal son, Ruth and Naomi.

I was and am supposed to be working on another manuscript, about the importance of prayer, praise and worship in our lives, but as I woke that Sunday morning, God inspired me to write a book about lessons learnt, from the prodigal son, Ruth and Naomi, and their journeys of faith.

Usually, I will spend several days planning what will go into each chapter and the Bible verses, but God said we are going to write this book differently. I am going to direct you and you are going to type the thoughts which I place into your head.

As I wrote the first version of this paragraph, it was late Monday evening; I completed the first draft of the book on Tuesday morning, 48 hours from when I typed the first words on my laptop.

As I have worked on this book, I have had time to reflect on my own journey of faith. I have seen these two stories in different ways. I would never have put them together, which is why I know this book is inspired.

In the past, I did not see the connection between the story of Joshua going into the promised land, and crossing the Jordan River, and how that was linked to the story of Ruth and Naomi, and the promised Messiah, which would come through the family line.

As I reflect now, following the deaths of loved ones this year, I am able to understand, at a much deeper level, the joy we will experience when we will be reunited, with our loved ones, and say, "We're home at last, never to be parted again."

I am giving God thanks and praise, for the miracles he has done, and is doing in my life. In the past, just one of these family deaths would have resulted in me spending several weeks in hospital, followed by months at home recuperating. This has not taken place this time, and we as a family thank God for His continued answers to prayers, for my health which God has continued to maintain.

I know without a shadow of a doubt, Father God is taking me on this journey, so I can be an encouragement to others, who are going through their own personal and professional challenges.

I would encourage you before you go to read the last chapter of this book, to take some time out and reflect on the journey you have been on, over the last few years, and the growth which has taken place in your life. When you do this, you too will ponder on the question, "**What is God asking me to do with my life?**

# CHAPTER 10

## *What Are Your Next Steps Going To Be?*

After the meeting, Boaz returned to the home of Ruth and Naomi and took Ruth to be his wife. They had a child; and they called his name Obed, which means worshiper.

When Obed was born, the women of the town said to Naomi, as recorded in **Ruth 4:14-15,**

*"Praise the LORD, who has now provided a redeemer for your family! May this child be famous in Israel. May he restore your youth and care for you in your old age. For he is the son of your daughter-in-law who loves you and has been better to you than seven sons!"*

Naomi then became the nurse for her grandson. Truly God had answered her prayers and given her an heir. Obed became the father of Jesse, who became the father of King David, an ancestor of Jesus Christ.

Perez was the father of Hezron, who was the father of Ram. Ram was the father of Amminadab, who was the father of Nahshon. Nahshon was the father of Salmon whose son was Boaz, the husband of Ruth.

If we fast track many generations and look at the genealogy of Jesus Christ in **Matthew Chapter 1:1-7**, once again we find Ruth and Boaz listed in His family line. We also find other women listed and the children they had.

Tamar whose sons were Perez and Zerah.

Rahab who was the mother of Boaz.

Ruth who was the mother of Obed.

If we look at the lives of these three women, each one of them had a special journey of faith. God made a way for each of them to be a distant relative of His Son. If you have time, go and research each of their stories, and it will give you encouragement to know that it's not how you start life, but what is important, is how you end it.

You should also be encouraged that God can take a nobody and make them a somebody. God can also take four women and their children and make them direct descendants of His Son. These situations were such that their actions could have cost them their lives, yet they displayed such great courage!

### God Has a Plan for Our Lives

For each of the women listed above, God had a plan for their lives. Judah had these twin boys in an unexpected way. Although Zerah put out his hand first at his birth and has a red cord tied around it, Perez was born first.

Rahab helped the two spies when they came to spy out Jericho. She made a pact with them that as she had saved their lives, when they came to destroy Jericho, they would spare her life and the lives of her family. The sign they were to look for, as to which house they were to preserve was be a scarlet cord hanging from the window.

Boaz would have been told the story of how his mother's life was preserved and therefore he would have understood the challenges Ruth faced when she came to Bethlehem. His mother, like Ruth was an foreigner.

Individually, each of these women's stories are remarkable but collectively, they show how amazing God is. They show the story of a God who loves his children dearly and will go out of His way to provide for their needs. They show He is a God who is forgiving and even when mistakes are made will use them for His good.

When we put these stories together with the story of the prodigal son, we get a truer picture of whom God is. A picture of a loving Father who wants intimate relationship with his children, and wants to bring out the greatness within their lives.

## What are Your Next Steps Going to Be?

Has your image of God changed while you have read this book? I know during the writing of this book; I have seen God in new ways. He has guided the various stories in this book each step of the way.

From a child my favourite text has been,

*"Trust in the LORD with all your heart, and lean not on your own understanding; In all your ways acknowledge Him, And He shall direct your paths."* **(Proverbs 3: 5-6, KJV).**

Some of the steps I have had to take, have been very painful and have caused my heart to break. I too, could have asked to be called Mara, like Naomi, when I have felt empty inside. There are other times God has taken challenges in my life and made then stepping stones to greater things. There are times when He has performed miracles, including the writing of this book, and my healing six years ago in May 2014.

I left home on a Friday afternoon in great pain and unable to walk unaided, to attend a retreat called **"Overcoming Emotional Baggage"**. Many would have stayed home, but something inside me, drove me to attend this retreat. Attending this retreat transformed my life, in ways I never would have thought possible.

I arrived on Friday lame, and went back on Sunday walking unaided and giving God thanks and praise. In the midst of praise and worship, healing took place. In the midst of praise and worship, my life was transformed in so many ways.

In the midst of praise and worship, a deeper intimate relationship began with Father God. I had to put my trust in him 100%. Ninety-nine percent would not do. You can read an account about what took place that weekend, in my devotional book, **"Listening for God's Voice: 40 Days of Developing Intimacy with God."**

## An Amazing Journey of Faith?

Rahab decided to protect the spies and she became the mother of Boaz.

Naomi and her family decided to go to Moab, because of the famine in Bethlehem, and Ruth becomes her daughter-in-law.

Ruth decided to come back with Naomi from Moab to Bethlehem.

Ruth and Boaz met, got married and had a child named Obed.

Obed became the father of Jesse.

Jesse became the father of King David.

Twenty-eight generations from King David, Jesus Christ is born to Mary whose husband was Joseph.

This journey started because Rahab heard and believed the stories she had heard about the God who looks after His children and performed miracles. She did not know her actions would have impacted the lives of others in such a remarkable way.

**Could it be that God has a plan for your life as He did with Rahab, or Ruth, or Boaz?**

**How Does This Relate to Your Journey of Faith?**

Where is God leading you? He has allowed you to read this book for a reason. What journey is He asking you to take? How does He want you to use your faith, and your life experiences?

Just like the prodigal son, or Ruth, Naomi or Boaz, there are people God wants you to meet. As you share your experiences, you can be the one to get them to start their own journey of faith.

There is a song which has a line that says, "It only takes a spark to get a fire going." One spark and a big fire can develop. A big fire can change a whole region. We have seen that happen literally.

As I typed this original line, there was a breaking news item on my phone. A fire, burning in the Notre

Dame Cathedral in Paris with fire-fighters battling to save the historic building. One spark destroyed the roof including the spire of an 850-year-old building, which will never be the same again.

The same way one spark transformed this historic building, God can allow the spark of the Holy Spirit to start burning brightly in your life. You will never be the same again. You will become transformed, like the changes which take place when a caterpillar becomes a butterfly. The caterpillar always has the butterfly within it, it just needs to be transformed. Part of this transformation, requires it to have a time of quietness, and seclusion away from others, so the greatness within can emerge.

You too need to have a time of quietness, and seclusion away from others, so the greatness within you too can emerge.

## Three Important Questions

I am going to end this book, by asking you the same three important questions, I asked at the start of the book. I think they are critical which is why I have repeated them three times in this book, the start, the middle and at the end. There is something profound when you ask the same question three times.

Often when you ask yourself a question the first time you will get a shallow answer. You may get a deeper answer the second time, but when you ask yourself a question when you have given yourself time and space to reflect and think things through carefully, you get a profound answer because you have to go much deeper inside of your thoughts.

**1.  How important is God in your life?**
**2.  Do you have a personal relationship with God?**
**3.  Where are you planning to spend eternity?**

Your answer to these questions will determine your final destiny. They will determine where your final home will be.

Do you now have a better picture of God? Can you now see He is the Father in the story of the prodigal son? Do you know He is the one running towards us, you and me, and each one of His sons and daughters, with open arms to welcome us back home?

God knows none of us are perfect, but that does not stop Him wanting us to be home with Him. He does not want us to focus on our past, but on our future. He wants us to have a good relationship with Him. Do you accept this will only happen if you see Him as a loving Father?

He does not only want this relationship to take place only here on earth. He is preparing a great celebration for us, in heaven, and He wants us all to attend.

You have a choice whether you will attend or not, just like the eldest son in the story of the prodigal son. God will ask you to attend the celebration, but He will not force you because He has given you free choice. He also does not want you to be living in a place where you will not be happy.

I am making preparations to be at the great celebration, and I hope you are too. I am looking forward to when I can say, "**I AM HOME AT LAST!**"

**How about you?**

# Conclusion

"This is my command—be strong and courageous! Do not be afraid or discouraged. For the LORD your God is with you wherever you go,"*(Joshua 1:9).*

### Crossing the River Jordan

Joshua is now the new leader, and he knows he has the responsibility of taking the children of Israel across the River Jordan, to occupy their new home in Canaan.

Just as preparations needed to be made when the Children of Israel left Egypt in the first Passover night, preparations needed to be made for this journey too. He reminded them *"The Lord your God is giving you a place of rest. He has given you this land,"* (**Joshua 1:13).**

Early in the morning on the third day, Joshua sent officers throughout the camp to let everyone know they will be crossing over the Jordan to the land in the East. Everyone gathered at the place where they were going to cross over, with the priest carrying the Ark of the Covenant in front.

Joshua said to the priests,

*"Lift up the Ark of the Covenant and lead the people across the river. When you reach the bank of the River Jordan, take a few steps into the river and stop there,"* (**Joshua 3:6b, 7c**).

He continued to share with the people,

*"As soon as the priests' feet touch the water, the flow of water will be cut off upstream, and the river will stand up like a wall,"* (**Joshua 3:13**).

This was the second time Joshua was experiencing such a miracle. He had crossed over on dry land, when the Red Sea parted, when they had left Egypt, and now he was crossing over on dry land again, this time, when the River Jordan parted.

**New Heaven and a New Earth**

Just as the Children of Israel went on their journey from Egypt to Canaan, the land God had promised Abraham his descendants would inherit as their home, we too are on a journey to our eternal home.

Our journey starts on earth, but after Jesus' Second Coming, will we live in mansions in heaven, as we read in **John 14:2 (NKJV),**

*"In My Father's house are many mansions, if it were not so, I would have told you. I go to prepare a place for you."*

123

But heaven will not be our final home. We read in **Revelations 21:1-4,**

*"Then I saw a New Heaven and a New Earth, for the old heaven and the old earth had disappeared. And the sea was also gone. And I saw the Holy City, the New Jerusalem, coming down from God out of heaven like a bride beautifully dressed for her husband. I heard a loud shout from the throne, saying, "Look, God's home is now among his people! He will live with them, and they will be His people. God Himself will be with them. He will wipe every tear from their eyes, and there will be no more death or sorrow or crying or pain. All these things are gone forever."*

When we occupy this home, we will be able to finally say, "**HOME AT LAST!**"

**Everlasting Life!**

In **John 3**, we read about a discussion which took place between Jesus and Nicodemus. Nicodemus knew Jesus had come from God, because of the many signs and miracles he had seen Him perform. He wanted to know, what did he need to do, in order to have a place in the kingdom of God.

He wanted to know what he needed to do to live in one of these mansions.

Jesus told him, he needed to be born again. He needed a fresh start.

The famous verse in the book of John, was shared with Nicodemus by Jesus as they spoke about what it means to be born again and gaining the gift of eternal life.

*"For God so loved the world that He gave His only begotten Son, that whoever believes in Him should not perish but have everlasting life,"* **John 3:16 (*KJV*).**

### God's Promises

When you observe the many challenges happening in the world which no one seems to have solutions, compounded with problems in your own personal life, where do you go for strength and support?

When you are all alone with your pain and many anxious thoughts are swirling around in your head, how do you cope?

For me, I have learnt to hold fast to the promises found in God's Word. It was not always like that, if I am being totally honest.

Over the years I have learnt to build a real intimate relationship with Father God, which includes reading and claiming the many promises, found in the Bible.

There are occasions when I do not have an answer, and do not know what to do. In the past I would have become anxious. But now, if I am still and listen carefully, I am reassured by God's comforting words found in the Bible.

Father God reminds me, just as He was with Joshua when he took his journey of faith, He will be with me and with all of us who want to build an everlasting relationship with Him, as we too go on our own journey of faith.

## What is Faith?

"*Now faith is the substance of things hoped for, and the evidence of things not seen.*" **Hebrews 11:1.**

**Hebrews Chapter 11** is known as the faith chapter. In this chapter we read about many individuals whose faith transformed not just their life, but the lives of others.

God wants us to have faith in Him, because it shows we love Him, trust Him, and want to have a lasting relationship with Him.

Hebrews Chapter 11, lists the names of many individuals, not groups, who were chosen for a particular role in history.

*"For many are called but few are chosen."* **(Matthew 22:14).**

## Who are Some of These Individuals Listed?

By faith **Abel** offered God a more excellent sacrifice than Cain, (v4).

By faith **Enoch** was taken away so he did not see death, (v5).

By faith **Noah** built an ark which saved his family, when the flood came, (v7).

By faith **Abraham** listened to the voice of God to go on a journey to receive the Promised Land as an inheritance, for his descendants, he did not know the route or how to find it, (v8).

By faith **Sarah** became a mother at the age of 90, when she was past child-bearing, (v11).

By faith, **Moses'** life was preserved as a baby. He refused to be called the son of Pharaoh's daughter, and later was used by God to lead the children of Israel out of Egypt to the Promised land, (v24).

The list goes on and on. It mentions other individuals who overcame challenges by faith, or the actions of others which are symbolic of their faith journey.

You have seen, how faith caused the **prodigal son** to return home to His Father, and how his life was transformed.

You have seen, how the decision of **Ruth** to go to Bethlehem with **Naomi**, caused her life and that of many others to be transformed.

By faith, **Ruth** the author of this book, has been on her own journey of faith which has transformed her life. She shares her transformation in many ways, as her own personal testimonies, to encourage others that they too can go on a similar journey, to get to know God in a personal and intimate way.

By faith (*place your name here*) …. In what ways are God using your life to transform others? What ways are you being a good witness for Him, in your circle of influence?

**God's Promises**

Before any major event takes place, God shares his plans with his leaders. He shared with **Moses and Aaron**, what would happen the night of the Passover, so the people could get ready and be prepared.

He shared with **Joshua**, what preparations needed to take place, so the children of Israel, could cross over the Jordan River safely, to go into Canaan.

He shared with **Noah**, what preparation needed to take place before the flood came, so he and his family would be saved.

**God is the same yesterday, today, and forever.**

We can be encouraged by the words found in **Amos 3:7**

*"Indeed, the sovereign LORD never does anything until he reveals His plans to His servants the prophets."*

We are also told in **Malachi 4:5,**

*"Look, I am sending you the prophet Elijah before the great and dreadful day of the Lord arrives. His preaching will turn the hearts of the fathers to their children, and the hearts of the children to their fathers. Otherwise I will come and strike the land with a curse."*

Let us use this time, we have at home, to build meaningful relationships with our families. Let us also use this time to get to know God in a more intimate way. This is our time of preparation. This is our time in the wilderness.

The children of Israel did not remain in the wilderness forever, as they had a destination they were going to.

We don't need to remain in this wilderness, we too have a destination we are going to, an eternal home.

I am looking forward to that day, when I will be reunited with my family and friends, who have died, as I know we will never have to part again.

I am also looking forward to the covenant God made with His children being fulfilled.

What about you?

What are you looking forward to?

Let your life be a journey of faith, until you are able to say, **" I AM HOME AT LAST!"**

**Amen and Amen!**

# The Prodigal's Song

Here I am, Sitting all alone;

How did I get here?

I had it all, but I let it go;

Now I'm wondering why, did I do so?


Here I am, in my home alone;

How did I get here?

I had it all, but it was taken away

Now I'm wondering how long, Will I stay here?


Should I stay, or should I go?

Are the questions that's in my mind

Will I be loved, or rejected again?

Dear Lord, can you hear my prayer?

# Home at Last

Here I am walking all alone,

How did I get here?

The journey is long, but I'm determined to go.

To see my Father, as I love Him so!


Here I am walking all alone,

How did I get here?

The journey is long, but I'm determined to go.

To see my Child, as I love them so!


Here I am, and I'm not alone

How did I get here?

I'm being embraced in my Father's arms

And it's so good to see, His loving face!


Words and Music by Ruth Pearson © 2020

## About the Author

**Ruth Pearson** is an inspirational teacher, lay pastor, motivational speaker and author who utilises her own personal experiences to empower others so that they too can develop an intimate relationship with Father God. She is also an accredited Master Coach, Conflict Resolution and Holistic Wellbeing trainer and qualified mediator. She is the founder of Listening to Your Voice Publishing.

Ruth has a vision to see people grow spiritually, intellectually, emotionally, and socially, whilst maximising their God-given potential. She is passionate about supporting others to develop an intimate relationship with Father God, as they have a truer picture of who He is. They will confidently know, **God is Love**.

Ruth Pearson has a vision to establish a network of collaborative services that will assist others in all areas of their life. These services will be modelled on the example shown in **Acts 6**, in the Bible, where everyone looked after the needs of each other, when the early church was established. Each member of these group then became equipped with the skills needed to become good Ambassador for Christ, sharing their own experiences, and journey of faith with others.

Ruth Pearson is available to preach, coach and train in the areas of motivation, wellbeing, leadership or conflict resolution, or be a keynote speaker, here in the United Kingdom, where she resides, and internationally.

She speaks about issues and themes related to empowering individuals to be the best they can be, despite any challenging situations they may face, so their lives can be transformed. She also supports others in practical ways, answering  deeper questions they may have about their relationship with Father God and His place in their lives.

She can be contacted via social media or her websites: www.listeningtoyourvoice.co.uk or www.ruthpearsonuk.com/

## Services

- Preaching
- Keynote speaking

- Discipleship coaching and training
- Wellbeing coaching and training
- Leadership coaching and training

- Conflict resolution training
- Mediation training
- Mediation services

- Book writing coaching
- Book Publishing

# Reflection Time

Use this page to write a love letter to Father, sharing your inner thoughts.

------------------------------------------------

------------------------------------------------

------------------------------------------------

------------------------------------------------

------------------------------------------------

------------------------------------------------

------------------------------------------------

------------------------------------------------

------------------------------------------------

------------------------------------------------

------------------------------------------------

------------------------------------------------

# Reflection Time

Use this page to write a love letter to Father, sharing your inner thoughts.

---------------------------------------------------------

---------------------------------------------------------

---------------------------------------------------------

---------------------------------------------------------

---------------------------------------------------------

---------------------------------------------------------

---------------------------------------------------------

---------------------------------------------------------

---------------------------------------------------------

---------------------------------------------------------

---------------------------------------------------------

---------------------------------------------------------

---------------------------------------------------------

# Reflection Time

Use this page to write a love letter to
Father, sharing your inner thoughts.

------------------------------------------------------------

------------------------------------------------------------

------------------------------------------------------------

------------------------------------------------------------

------------------------------------------------------------

------------------------------------------------------------

------------------------------------------------------------

------------------------------------------------------------

------------------------------------------------------------

------------------------------------------------------------

------------------------------------------------------------

------------------------------------------------------------

------------------------------------------------------------

# Reflection Time

Use this page to write a love letter to
Father, sharing your inner thoughts.

------------------------------------------------------------

------------------------------------------------------------

------------------------------------------------------------

------------------------------------------------------------

------------------------------------------------------------

------------------------------------------------------------

------------------------------------------------------------

------------------------------------------------------------

------------------------------------------------------------

------------------------------------------------------------

------------------------------------------------------------

------------------------------------------------------------

------------------------------------------------------------

# Reflection Time

Use this page to write a love letter to
Father, sharing your inner thoughts.

----------------------------------------------------------------

----------------------------------------------------------------

----------------------------------------------------------------

----------------------------------------------------------------

----------------------------------------------------------------

----------------------------------------------------------------

----------------------------------------------------------------

----------------------------------------------------------------

----------------------------------------------------------------

----------------------------------------------------------------

----------------------------------------------------------------

----------------------------------------------------------------

# Reflection Time

Use this page to write a love letter to
Father, sharing your inner thoughts.

------------------------------------------------------------

------------------------------------------------------------

------------------------------------------------------------

------------------------------------------------------------

------------------------------------------------------------

------------------------------------------------------------

------------------------------------------------------------

------------------------------------------------------------

------------------------------------------------------------

------------------------------------------------------------

------------------------------------------------------------

------------------------------------------------------------

------------------------------------------------------------

"For I know the plans I have for you," says the Lord.

"They are plans for good and not for disaster, to give you a future and a hope. In those days when you pray, I will listen." (Jeremiah 29: 11-12)

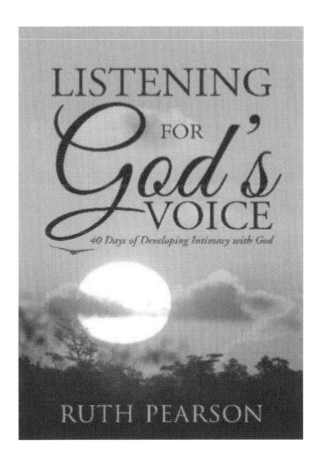

In a world of constant noise, it is no surprise that many of us struggle to tune in to hear what God has to say to us. Yet, God is very interested in every detail of our lives. He still speaks.

Do you believe that God can communicate with you today as He did with Eve, Abraham, Samuel, and Moses?

In this devotional that shares personal experiences and life lessons learnt from biblical characters and nature.

Ruth Pearson encourages the reader to have a more intimate relationship with Father God. Her prayer is that you will be renewed and transformed by developing Your own personal relationship with Father as you listen for His voice.

"Listen to your inner voice, and do not let anyone stop you from being the person you know within, you need to be."

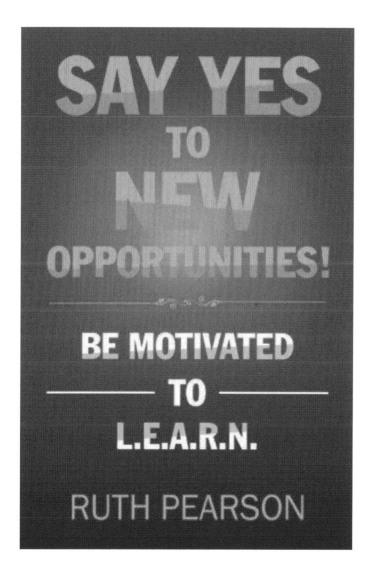

When life throws a curveball, it can knock you off your feet, and it may take you only seconds or minutes to get up. But sometimes, it takes hours, days, months, or years and you could stay down.

When Ruth Pearson suffered an emotional breakdown while teaching, she felt as though her life had fallen apart. After twenty-five years, she was afraid to go back into a classroom.

No matter what you do for a living, you know how hard it can be to overcome personal and professional problems.

Get the inspiration you need to accomplish your goals and conquer your fears with the lessons in *Say Yes to New Opportunities*!